19 95

Malcolm Morley: Paintings 1965-82

D1240328

Malcolm Morley: Paintings 1965-82

MALCOLM MORLEY

Paintings 1965-82

The Whitechapel Art Gallery

1983

The exhibition
is organised by the Whitechapel Art Gallery
and shown at the following venues:

Basel
22 January – 27 February 1983
Kunsthalle

Rotterdam
17 April – 29 May 1983
Museum Boymans van Beuningen

London
22 June – 21 August 1983
The Whitechapel Art Gallery

Washington, DC
9 September – 6 November 1983
Corcoran Gallery of Art

Chicago
19 November 1983 – 22 January 1984
Museum of Contemporary Art

New York
18 February – 15 April 1984
The Brooklyn Museum

The exhibition in London is sponsored by
Sotheby's

The Whitechapel Art Gallery,
an independent charitable trust,
is most grateful for the regular financial assistance
which it receives from
The Arts Council of Great Britain,
The Greater London Council,
The Inner London Education Authority,
The Greater London Arts Association,
and the London Boroughs of Tower Hamlets
and Hackney

Contents

Lenders

Janne and Carl Christian Aegidius, Paris
Bo Alveryd, Kävlinge, Sweden
Bud Bernstein, Birmingham, Michigan
Magnus Bromander, Göteborg
Jean Christophe Castelli, New York
Xavier Fourcade Inc, New York
Mr and Mrs Richard Hedreen, Seattle, Washington
Nancy Hoffman, New York
Paul and Camille Oliver-Hoffmann, Charlottesville, Virginia
Jack H. Klein, New York
Sydney and Frances Lewis, Richmond, Virginia
Martin Z. Margulies, Coconut Grove, Florida
Larry and Cindy Meeker, Kansas City, Kansas
Robert Miller Gallery, New York
Mr and Mrs Morton Neuman, Chicago
Doris and Charles Saatchi, London
Jacqueline and Julian Schnabel, New York
Stanley J. Seeger, Sutton Place, Guildford, England
Robert B. Shapiro, Skokie, Illinois
Klaus and Anneliese Wolf, Essen
Private collections

Ludwig Collection, Neue Galerie, Aachen
Museum of Contemporary Art, Chicago
Louisiana Museum of Modern Art, Humlebaek, Denmark
The Metropolitan Museum of Art, New York
Munson-Williams-Proctor Institute, Utica, New York
Museum van Hedendaagse Kunst, Utrecht
Ludwig Stiftung, Museum Moderner Kunst, Vienna

Acknowledgments

An exhibition which is to be shown in six cities on two continents can only take place with the understanding and close cooperation of owners. In the case of the Morley exhibition most of those approached have recognised the importance of the event and have been extremely generous in allowing us to borrow paintings for a sixteen month period. May I extend my thanks on behalf of the collaborating institutions and the many visitors who will see the exhibition during its tour.

May we also thank Michael Compton, Keeper of Exhibitions and Education at the Tate Gallery, London for his introduction to and commentary on Morley's work. The paintings are dispersed, making his task especially difficult, and we are grateful for the trouble which he has taken.

The artist's dealer in New York, Xavier Fourcade, and the staff of Xavier Fourcade Inc, Margaret Parker and Jill Weinberg, have given generous assistance at all stages in the preparation of the exhibition which has involved the compilation of a full record of Morley's paintings. Amongst others who have given advice at critical moments may I also thank Gail McAdoo, Daryl Harnisch and Valentin Tatransky.

Throughout our preparations we have benefited from the close collaboration of Malcolm Morley. He has made available his archives and has spent many hours discussing the project. Without this assistance the project could never have been realized in its present fullness.

The exhibition in London is sponsored by Sotheby's. The Whitechapel welcomes this support for the contemporary arts and in particular thanks Lucy Havelock-Allan of Sotheby's contemporary department for her interest.

Foreword

Although Malcolm Morley is now fifty and has been painting for nearly thirty years this is not a retrospective exhibition of the kind conventionally given to painters in mid-career. We have chosen to show only the development of his painting from the moment of his emergence as a distinct figure within the community of painters, omitting the early landscapes and abstract paintings as well as the watercolours and drawings which have more recently become an important part of his work. There will no doubt be other exhibitions devoted to these aspects, but for this first museum exhibition we felt that his central concerns needed to be to the fore.

Morley is not well known outside the close-knit world of New York painting, although there he is increasingly regarded as one of the principal figures of his generation. In twenty years he has shown only a handful a paintings in four mixed exhibitions in his native country, whilst an intermittent series of shows in New York and Europe has meant that almost no-one can have consistently followed his evolution. Paradoxically Morley has sold almost every picture he has painted and as these are now very widely dispersed it is even more difficult to grasp the complete range of his work. At the most simple level the exhibition will therefore offer information and allow comparisons to be made.

What, one might ask, are the qualities which make Morley's work so significant and which generate such interest on the part of other artists? I believe that respect is engendered in part by his relentless determination to probe the fundamental question which confronts all painters; that is, how does one represent, through the medium of brush and paint on a two-dimensional surface, the complexity of the visible world before us. Morley's own regard for Cézanne provides corroborative evidence of his commitment to this question, while his painstaking method of filling in the grid, square by square, to ensure equality of value for all areas of the canvas, is a practical demonstration. However, there are many dogged artists. What distinguishes Morley is not simply his ability to manipulate paint, or the quality of his painterly invention (just look at the range of handling within any recent canvas) or even his fresh and often subtle use of brilliant colour. It is the power of his imagination.

Morley's paintings are not programmes but free associations which grow in the mind of the painter. The painter establishes the fragments which then become open territory for personal interpretation by the viewer. At different times Morley has drawn together childhood memories and our common fear of twentieth-century forms of death through train and air crashes. He has united arcadian or paradise landscapes with the horrors of modern warfare. In Morley's world symbols frequently establish links between modern and ancient cultures, and imagination touches not fantasy but the collective unconscious of contemporary life.

Nicholas Serota

Director, Whitechapel Art Gallery

Malcolm Morley
Michael Compton

The apparent style of the paintings of Malcolm Morley has ranged from the faithful rendering of photographic images in his ships of 1965 to the violent drama of the early 'seventies and the free painterliness of recent works. However, it would be quite wrong to think that there was any generic difference in the degree of urgency, emotional intensity or autobiography between these groups. They are not only all from the same hand but they represent the continuous evolution of a working method and of personal as well as artistic maturity.

Morley was born, brought up and trained as an artist in England but, on leaving the Royal College, moved immediately to New York. He is of average height but rather stocky and of a powerful physique, which can appear threatening. His manner is genial, sometimes self-deprecating, but obviously competitive. He tells stories of his own aggressive behaviour and response to others whom he feels have not behaved reasonably. He sees himself, like Hemingway, as challenging directly the dominating figures of the art world. He may have settled in New York because that was where the champions lived. There is a general sense of competition in art, as in commerce, the academic fields and almost every aspect of life. He is not afraid of recognising heroes, or even mentors, among older artists and is delighted when it is pointed out that some attitude or device of his own has its precedents in the great art of the past. He is a little less comfortable when he is compared in the same way with contemporaries: he values his uniqueness.

Morley's generation at the Royal College was that of the first Pop artists (following the proto-Pop of Richard Hamilton and Eduardo Paolozzi) but he himself evolved as an abstract artist under the influence of the great Americans including De Kooning and Rothko who had been shown in London at the Tate Gallery in 1956 and 1959. He switched to painting from mass-media models only in the mid-'sixties and what he then produced can be seen as both a culmination, an extreme form of Pop art, and as a prototype of Photo-realism. His art was not itself photo-realist, but, when that movement came briefly to a phase of extreme commercial exploitation, Morley was already pursuing a development all his own. This can be considered as a forerunner of much modern 'wild' painting, even if he shares little with the exponents of that fancy. However, he is not inclined to boast of any priority or leading role.

This brief sketch of a character study is intended to illuminate obliquely a curious feature of Morley's art, which is that his most extreme innovations have often been the result of an equally extreme caution, itself closely associated with his own anxieties.

Morley's early work in New York was strongly influenced by that of the great painters De Kooning and Barnett Newman, who nurtured many young artists by their example and generosity. There are, in Morley's oeuvre, as in the De Kooning series of the 'forties, white paintings and black. He was caught up in the classical preoccupations of the picture surface and of the painted mark. He devised a variety of means of making marks on the surface, including the use of icing nozzles, which determined not only the extension but the cross-sections of the strokes. His reality was the painterly gesture which might be as regular as practised calligraphy or as irregular as graffiti. Such a picture as **High July** (1964) is divided into horizontal bands, figured in loops and waves like cake decorations in icing sugar and textured in the same way. He met Barnett Newman while waiting on him at a restaurant table and was encouraged by this hero who, characteristically, came to his studio and complimented him on the light in his paintings. His appreciation and advice were metaphoric – he did not wish to tell young artists what to do – least of all to imitate his own style.

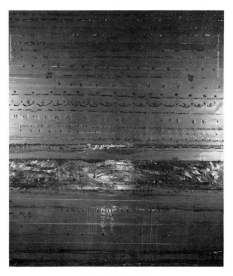

Untitled c.1963

Morley's last abstract picture had four strips of a photograph of a ship hanging from the lower edge. The structural sculptor, Mark di Suvero, advised him to clean the dirt from his studio window and paint what was outside – the ships. Morley did not quite do this. He turned to what had been a childhood preoccupation – warships. He had been at a naval school (from which he had been expelled) and had made scale models of famous warships. He was to recall later, under psycho-analysis, that the last of these, finished and waiting to be painted, had stood on the window-sill of his house which was destroyed that night in World War II by a V-bomb. Morley escaped, but was evacuated and ceased to make such models.

His first ship paintings were in greys, like the warships themselves. Following the practise of Richard Artschwager, he floated ink on the surface, which dried in spots in the interstices of the canvas to produce a texture analogous to the silk screen of Andy Warhol, or the dots of Roy Lichtenstein.

However, the finest ships that Morley could see on the river and at the piers of Manhattan were the Atlantic liners and cruise ships. He attempted to paint one from the dock-side, but it was much too large, towering above him and extending far on either side. It could not be painted without moving his head and body and dissolving the unity of the picture plane. He made a mess, but he thought he might be able to deal with something much smaller. Accordingly, he obtained postcards and brochures from shipping offices, and, using a traditional technique, he divided a postcard into a grid of eight parts each way in order to transform it, section by section, into a large painting. This practise has become a central component of Morley's technique and is not only a convenient device but is embedded in the purpose and meaning of his work.

Regular grids had been used by the ancient Egyptians to govern the proportions of figures and to guarantee their orthodoxy. Figures carved or painted could be created on any relative or absolute scale by varying the units of the grid. The Greeks used measures as a device for endowing figures with the beauty and harmony of mathematical proportions. Grids continued to be employed for similar reasons by artists and architects throughout the Middle Ages. With the invention (or reinvention) of single viewpoint perspective, they could be used both to regulate the composition and to associate scale with distance. Well-known woodcuts by Dürer (dating from c.1527), show artists observing a motif through a picture plane of crossed threads which correspond to grids drawn on their sheets of paper. The function of such a grid is not only to scale the image up or down but to divide the field of vision into small areas, regular enough to locate elements accurately. A further result of using a grid is that by breaking up the natural configurations, it can correct the habit of the eye and mind of perceiving the world in terms of what they 'know' rather than what they see.

However, all this history, (as well as the use of grids by twentieth century artists like Bomberg or Van Doesburg as motifs or regulators of their composition) was virtually unknown to Morley at the time. What he did know were the grids of Artschwager, who used them as a means of replicating images on a chosen scale; of Agnes Martin and Robert Ryman, who made them as an essential, visible structure of their work. He also know those of Warhol, who used them as a metaphor of mindless repetition, and of Carl Andre and other Minimalists, who used them to reduce forms to the point where they merely defined the unit of production and rid the com-

Albrecht Dürer:
Woodcut c.1527

position of any quasi-linguistic structure. Chuck Close was to employ grids in a way nearer to that of traditional squaring-up.

Curiously, Morley's grids functioned in a spirit closer to those historical uses which he did not know than to the current ones that he did know. The point of the grid for him was precisely to divide the model – that is the experience – into manageable bits. It is as if, entering a new realm of art, he meant to take the smallest and even the most tentative steps. In principle, he would go back to a device that he had learned from his teacher, Philip Matthews, at Camberwell School of Art in the early 'fifties. Faced with the problem of matching a tone among many adjacent tones in the field of vision, he had been shown that it could be isolated and made independent of its context, by being looked at through a hole in a piece of card. In its extreme form, Morley's method involved scanning the model, section by section, through a succession of such rectangular apertures and then matching what he saw in the corresponding rectangles of a canvas already divided proportionately and neutrally tinted.

Morley was able to complete each rectangle as an entity, independent of the rest, just as a fresco painter paints his daywork before the plaster dries. Now this is not for Morley a purely mechanical process. When he began, he used it in a partially compromised way, allowing the work to spread in threads over the edges of the rectangle, so as to make the matching of the next one easier. He also painted separately elements that were, in fact, separate, but in the original postcards merely different proportions of the same inks. That is, for example, the sea and the hull of the ship. The divisions of 'experience' into parcels of generally equal and small proportions was an expression of his anxiety about handling it whole and unstructured. He did not want to 'bite off more than he could chew'. At the same time, it was an allegory of independence. In spite of the apparently mechanical nature of the task, the processes allowed Morley to make each decision on the placing of a particle of colour independently of others but in a spirit of fidelity to the model.

Fidelity is a word that Morley has come to find more appropriate than say, precision, exactitude, imitation or realism. The tenuous link with human, even sexual, relations seems appropriate. In the past he has gone further and referred to the 'pornography' of a painting. That is, 'paint' is a two-dimensional thing capable of arousing but not fulfilling the desire of the three-dimensional body of the viewer. Such an interpretation would be a bizarre way to describe the austere search for two-dimensional reality as it was articulated by the critic Clement Greenberg. However, the content of Morley's paintings makes it fitting to consider his work in these sexual terms. Moreover it seems to me perfectly justifiable for us to go further in associating meanings with the work than ever the artist was conscious of at the time. For an example among an almost indefinite number, the word 'pornography' comes from the ancient Greek word used to describe prostitutes. Both the ship and the sea are classically 'women'. Morley's ships are 'cruise' ships, they offer pleasure without other purpose. The picture – the ship – is sold for pleasure, etc. Morley would not repudiate any interesting meaning or association even though, for him, the work has its own specific private meaning. That meaning is partly autobiographical, he had been a seaman on a cargo ship and had aspired to work on a grand ocean liner. He had come to America on such a ship. His ships have great names, signifying heroic and glamorous figures and places, **Leonardo da Vinci, Empire Monarch, United States,** etc. They symbolise an ordered and protected shell against the wild environment of the sea. They are going somewhere or arriving. All this, together with the ordering of sensation, is part of the available meaning.

There is also a range of meaning which derives from the art historical problematic of the day to which I have already partly referred. This is the matter of support, medium and illusion. Morley's work follows in the wake of Abstract Expressionism, which could be considered a means of eliminating another degree of illusionism. He also followed Robert Rauschenberg and Jasper Johns, who had attached or assembled three-dimensional and painted flat objects to get around the 'problem' of illusion. After them, Lichtenstein and Warhol had processed flat but powerful images into paintings by changing the scale, medium, etc., so making pictures of what were already conventional flat objects, comic strips or newspaper pictures in half-tone. However, Morley's paintings, although reconstruct-

Empire Monarch 1965

ed from two-dimensional models, create an inescapable sense of three dimensions. In fact it is precisely the accuracy of the two-dimensional projection – the grid – and the completeness of the two-dimensional surface – the paint layer – that guarantee the third dimension.

Morley's pictures also bring in train the sequence of transformations of idea, picture and object that lies behind the apparently simple photographic image that he has chosen. The story, in brief, goes as follows: a person (or rather a group of people) have an idea for a ship (that is, effectively, a picture of a ship) in their minds. They pay someone to make a design for it: a prescriptive series of drawings of every part. This detailed picture is then converted into a 'real' ship, by means of a whole array of paid skills and crafts. The ship is painted (that is, it is coated in coloured paint according to certain conventions and usages): the painting is heraldic, seductive and protective. It is itself a 'picture'. An advertising agent will procure photographs, taken according to certain conventions – each one will be a 'picture' in the minds of owners, agents and photographers. From these, one is selected on the criterion of expression (it is likely to attract customers) and processed for printing. The printed image is, like the photograph, a pigmented skin on a surface which is distributed and then chosen by Morley to be used by him as a surrogate for, or manifestation of, his own desires, in the form of a skin of paint on a canvas.

Although Morley has anxieties about his work, they centre on a possible failure of his continuing desire to paint, not on whether the picture will succeed. 'Success' is guaranteed both by the method described above and by the fact that any mark that has been made is automatically accepted by the artist. He does not, in principle, make corrections. A gross example of this approach is that, having miscalculated the proportion of the canvas for **Empire Monarch** he simply painted the extra part black – he did not cut off the excess.

Morley frequently painted (and has continued to paint) these pictures upside down partly so as to defeat the tendency to paint ready-made formulations of such familiar concepts as a wavy sea. The device was helpful because the strong illusionism of the model was more difficult to escape from than, for example, the already formalised images used by Lichtenstein. The same device has its poignancy if one considers that, of all great natural phenomena, it is the sea, with its horizon, which most strongly distinguishes up from down.

Morley uses no devices to flatten the image, which is as real as the reprographic process can make it, only more powerful both because it is much larger and because it is presented for special attention by virtue of being a work of art. However there is a limit to the point for point fidelity of the painting; when looked at very close up it is seen to be made, not of the dots of the half-tone reprographic screen but of minute ordered, abstract strokes. It turns out to be, in form as well as in substance, a painting, but, precisely because it has this character, not a photo-realist painting. Although the brush stroke, the agent of the artist's psychological and somatic expression, is on the smallest possible scale, it makes up for this proportionately by number and insistence. Such paintings took months to complete and, looking closely, it is possible to imagine the high degree of commitment thay they involved. No wonder his anxieties took the form of doubt that he could continue to paint, of fears of impotence. It is as if such a picture was, in addition to its other roles, a test of his own sustained arousal. In this respect one is reminded of the large paintings of Seurat.

SS Amsterdam in Front of Rotterdam 1966

Several such pictures were painted by Morley in 1965-66. The most completely successful and the one in which the method was most strictly applied is the **SS Amsterdam in Front of Rotterdam**. This painting has strong diagonals converging on a vanishing point outside the picture to the right (like many Dutch riverscapes). It has a feature, absent from the earliest ships described above, that is, a white border. The purpose of this is to bring the junction between the illusion and the field into the picture instead of leaving it to take place, in a less controlled way, at the edge, where it may be affected by the thickness of the canvas, the frame, a shadow on the wall, etc. It functions like the cards with rectangular apertures described above. But, of course, the margin may also be an image of the paper or card on which the model is printed and is just as much an illusion as the ship, the sea, or anything else represented in the picture.

On Deck 1966

There are two further pictures of the same size, but upright in format, which represent the ship from within – **Ships's Dinner Party** and **On Deck**. The models used in the picture had for Morley a slightly Germanic look (the ship was, in fact, Dutch) and are in a scale which is so grossly enlarged from the printed image that they appear unaturally frozen. The braceletted and black-gloved hand projecting into the centre has an unmistakeably fetishistic presence, emphasised by the black-sleeved forearm of the man on the right.

Like Lichtenstein, Morley moved to fine art reproduction for the model of his picture, **Vermeer, Portrait of the Artist in his Studio**. This painting is plainly selected because of its connections into Morleys own practise. The original by Vermeer shows the artist from behind, painting a picture of a posed, allegorical model beyond a plane defined by a figured curtain, which could be pulled across to block the view. On the wall in the background is another form of representation, a map surrounded with en-

graved views of Dutch cities, often seen from the sea or river and so resembling to this degree the settings of Morley's own cruise liners. Vermeer is a painter whose apparently seamless and dispassionate objectivity is found, on close inspection, to be marked by highly personal and distinct, if minute, touches of the brush.

Race Track 1970

Having gone so far, Morley could easily have continued to produce a uniform or slowly developing kind of painting which would have had a secure market, especially in view of the success of Photo-realism. But Morley works without regard for such questions and his art changed, though not in a direction which one might have expected. The dramatic first step was manifested in the painting **Race Track**. This picture of horses galloping to the line in front of a grandstand was in its way the most ambitious of the high fidelity paintings I have been describing. Like most of them, it was a high-life subject drawn from an advertising picture, in fact, a poster. What made it distinctive was the immense number of people it contained, each painted individually. It took many months to complete and, with its cast of thousands, it put Morley in the position of Cecil B. de Mille. The critic Nicolas Calas said to Morley: 'Jasper Johns began by painting flags, now he paints flag-stones' (exact words not guaranteed!). Morley took this as a hint and turned the picture into an unambiguously political one – the extreme instance in his oeuvre up to this date. It took the form of a gesture at once obvious to the point of banality and more subtly disturbing: disturbing in terms of his art.

The race track in question was, as it happens, in South Africa and specifically at Greyville. The puns on race and colour were too clear to miss. Morley had a signwriter paint the lettering on the white surround, having covered up the image. He also decided to paint an apparently violent, red cross (a reference to the black activist Malcolm X and a mark of dissent to the society represented) over the picture. It was a gesture of sacrifice but he went about it in a characteristically careful way – he could not yet bring himself to paint a brush stroke as large and sweeping as was necessary and he was genuinely reluctant to cover up any large part of what he had already done. Accordingly, he painted a lar-

Ship's Dinner Party 1966

Vermeer, Portrait of the Artist in his Studio 1968

ge, but thin, cross on a sheet of plastic, and he turned it round, back and forth until he had found the right position, right, that is, in terms of the formal division of the canvas into segments. Then the plastic was pressed-down hard onto the canvas, transferring the paint to it as one does in monotype. The paint squeezed out sideways, obliterating rather more of the canvas than Morley had intended.

There is a reversal here: while he had been painting pictures of printed images by means of brushstrokes that could only be detected close to, he had now printed in paint a picture of a brush stroke that can only be distinguished as printing from close-up. He had made his gesture of political protest and, at the same time, he had renounced a style that had been effectively 'wasted' by the mass of photo-realists. As a political gesture, I think it must seem to its author to be rather simple, although, amazingly, the most obvious thing about it, the pun, 'race track' was overlooked by many.

At first, the minute physical gestures by means of which he executed his work and his disciplined use of the primary grid did not loosen. He did make a further gesture that was rather less dramatic. Having painted another postcard picture of Buckingham Palace he attached to it a gymkhana rosette and called it **Buckingham Palace with First Prize.** The joke is a little ambiguous, who had come first: Morley, the Horseguards riding past, or the Queen? Several years later, Morley felt the urge to give more point and drama to the joke. The picture was to be sold at auction in Paris. Morley, having started a rumour that something would take place so as to heighten expectancy, appeared at the sale in evening dress (Yves Klein's costume) armed with a realistic water-pistol, filled with red paint. He intended to write with it *'faux'* (fake) over the picture. The *maître-priseur* had taken the precaution of covering the painting with plastic sheeting, so, extemporising, as the picture was being removed in the hubbub, Morley nailed the pistol to it, allowing the 'blood' to spill-out and stain the edge of the canvas.

The classic case of an artist declaring his own work false is that of Giorgio de Chirico, but Morley wanted to put himself to the risk of being involved in a law-suit to determine to what degree an artist should be able to control his work after its sale. French law does acknowledge a continuance of the painter's artistic rights. However, I think this gesture was primarily another test of himself, related to his own anxieties. He recounts another such gesture, when, at a time when he was not able to sell work, having just sold a painting for $ 40,000, he slashed it to pieces in front of the new owner's eyes and handed back the cheque. It will be recognised that these demonstrations are related in type and mood to much that was going on under the name of Conceptual Art at the time.

New York City Postcard was made in response to a patron's request for a work of unusual proportions. Morley was able to find an image

to match, a concertina fold-out postcard of New York. This was sent to the patron and mailed back to Morley, who painted it in his usual way, including the handwritten address, again a touch of Conceptual Art. Equally in the spirit of that art was the larger version of this work, with an extra panel and constructed as a free-standing painting. If one side is put the right way up, the other (as in the model) is upside down. One may detect several little private jokes in what is one of Morley's biggest pictures. First, since he often painted upside down, (in order to avoid painting what he expected to see) the pictures which seemed to be the right way up were wrong (in relation to their construction) and *vice versa.* Second, (since he had been all along an abstract expressionist, painting images as a means of further delegating control to the medium) he was one of the few 'abstract' artists whose work would never be hung the wrong way up. Yet here, nearly half must always be 'upside down' and two are on edge! Third, some modernist sculpture of artists like David Smith and Anthony Caro was floor-related as well as painted.

In the works of the 'seventies a new concept, 'shift', became an important factor. Shift, specifically of viewpoint, has its history both in astronomy (parallax) and in art. It was a characteristic of Cubism and of Russian Futurism under the name *sdvig*, that Morley also uses. A dramatic 'shift' occurred by chance in one of Morley's paintings. Invited to do a college tutorial, he elected to perform Raphael's fresco, **The School of Athens** to the music of Monteverdi.

School of Athens 1972

But, in the event, as he was filling-in the prepared grid, he made a mistake and a whole file of squares was shifted one unit to the right, grotesquely taking off the tops of the heads of the philosophers, leaving them like so many boiled eggs. Morley decided to accept the mistake and incorporate it in his **School of Athens.** One may conjecture that the 'mistake' was adopted in this way party out of regard for the

tenets of Abstract Expressionism and Surrealism which respect the psycho-analytic theory of the significance of unconscious 'mistakes'. Furthermore, it fitted in with his own principle of working from what was given (which has been discussed above in the context of **Empire Monarch**). Morley's own self-portrait does not take the place of that of Raphael, but of Diogenes, reclining on the steps in the centre.

Los Angeles Yellow Pages 1971

By the early 'seventies, a decisive development in Morley's painting was manifesting itself. The key work is **Los Angeles Yellow Pages.** The model for this work was itself painterly, specifically a cover of the Los Angeles' Yellow Pages telephone directory that he had used as a palette. It comprised a half-tone image like those he had used before, with surrounding typography. Paint had been spread upon it and, where this had been peeled-off, it had picked up the printed skin of the paper. Some of this had been laid-down slightly awry and stuck-on with paint itself. In addition, the paper was torn and Morley drew two arcs with a protractor in homage to Jasper Johns. Morley treated this partly accidental artefact as a model, representing the smears of paint and the tear, but the scale of his brush stroke was growing into a form of hatching, proportional to the strokes of, say, an Impressionist in the 1870's. It is possible to see how he has matched the colour to the model, slightly differently in one independent instance than in the other. The indications of an approximately two-inch grid in red are left visible at the edges.

It can be seen that the illusion, which is in any case destroyed when one approaches close enough to see the brush strokes, is here subverted sooner, for the tear, which is black and

may appear convincing in one light, does not change as shadow should with shifts or changes in power in the light source. Nor does it alter with the colour of the source or background. Similarly its configuration is not distorted, as it should be, by shifting the point from which the picture is looked at.

The scale of the work is also significant. Up to this point Morley's scale had been similar to that of some of the Pop artists. That is, the model would generally represent something very large, such as a ship, but would be itself relatively small, such as a postcard. This would then be enlarged in painting by Morley until it reached the human, or superhuman scale typical also of Abstract Expressionism. Within this format Morley would work on the constant scale of his own craft, up to now, that of finger and minimal hand movements. It has been observed that when people write on a giant scale (perhaps, with their feet as they do when they write their names in the sand on a beach) they reproduce essentially the same patterns as they do when they write with minute actions of the fingers. Morley began to enlarge the scope of his movements from this date (1971), using first the hand more freely, and then his forearm, though his hand-writing remained virtually constant. The change affected the iconography by association. When scaled up, the 'accidents' of the brush strokes became visible. **Los Angeles Yellow Pages** is the result of various studio 'accidents' which were in turn allegorical of real-life accidents. Like them they were affected by historical and subconscious tendencies or intentions.

Piccadilly Circus 1973

Piccadilly Circus is a picture which began as a pastiche of the Abstract Expressionism of De Kooning in the period of, say, his *Attic* (1949) (to name a painting that included a newspaper image by offset). In the gaps between the very large and free strokes and splashes of paint, Morley represented a postcard of Piccadilly Circus. The effect was now deliberately a mess. The 'violence' of the 'Abstract Expressionism' in the picture seems to be transferred to the subject, so that at first sight it could be a vast traffic accident. (Piccadilly Circus had been recurrently the subject of development controversy and threatened also to be a planning 'accident').

This expressionist picture was also among the

first in which he reverted from acrylic, with its associations of dispassion, to oil, with its tradition of emotional expression. Moreover, this picture was completed by Morley hanging a bag of grey paint over it and having friends shoot arrows into that, so that the paint leaked, like grey blood, over the surface. The references of this action are obscure and ambivalent. On the one hand they point back again to Abstract Expressionism and even to Zen archery, often cited as a parallel to painterly behaviour. On the other hand, they signal the emotion of the break-up of Morley's marriage. It could be seen as displaced revenge; but he could not bring himself even to fire an arrow.

Without stretching the point too far, we may consider that **Belly** represents a personal accident. Morley acknowledges his own rotundity by superimposing his own double-chinned head onto his belly (his eyes were bigger than his belly). Reference is also made, obliquely, to Magritte's well-known *The Rape*. The picture is a classical self-portrait in a mirror, but the mirror is placed at an angle so that as he is on the point of shaving, Morley catches sight of his own stomach instead of his face. The paint strokes are quite large, approximating to those of, say, Rembrandt, whose self-portraits effectively define that motif. This picture, which stands a little apart from the main course of Morley's development, comprises two spaces, the 'real' space around the mirror, which divides the picture on the skew (like the cross in **Race Track**) and the virtual space, seen in the mirror, which nearly fills it, just as the looking-glass nearly fills the actual picture, surfeiting it.

The General is a painting that takes further the attack on the limitation of the two-dimensional subject. The 'model' for this picture was a wooden-edged children's slate onto which was stuck two forms of disturbed image. There were parts of two mixed-up, postcard-sized, jigsaws, whose discontinuous and mutually interrupted images may be considered as taking further the patchworked image of **Piccadilly Circus**. The central feature, however, is a crumpled postcard. The reference is to Cubism, for the paintings of Picasso and Braque of c.1909-11 can be considered as an attempt to create a notation for three-dimensional objects on the two dimensions of a canvas. This resulted in the appearance of facetting in their paintings. Morley scrambles the system and still gets a picture. His image (of a three-dimensional figure, Eisenhower) is reduced to two dimensions by the optics of the camera and then crumpled-up by Morley. When painted, using the optics of a grid (essentially identical to the camera), this appears as facets.

The painting contains more explicit political overtones than any before. It links war, the general and the painted gaiter formerly attached to the edge of the picture, with the gun mentality of the U.S.A. The picture was painted in Texas and has the gun of the west, the Winchester repeater, hanging over it on hooks made from horse shoes, such as are used by truck drivers

there. The slate itself was shot through with bullets and attached to the edge of the painting. The whole then contained the assaulted image of its model just as **Piccadilly Circus** does. At the top the rifle is powerless, unloaded; at the bottom hangs an empty holster and gun belt which had live cartridges in it – equally impotent but dangerous. (The slate and gaiter have subsequently been removed).

Ladies of Texas, exhibits Morley's preoccupation with violence but in a context which was more personal and through an imagery which is much less direct. Morley went as visiting artist to a college in Houston, where he took the role of a student in class. The instructor handed each student a copy of a photograph of a nude in a pin-up posture, saying 'You can do anything you like'. Morley, while he was pointedly asking for confirmation of the instruction, crumpled and tore his print into small pieces. He went on to fix them in a bag, which he roped up, turning it into the semblance of a sado-masochistic object. He used this as the model for his picture. For the background he used a poster advertising Cézanne's town, Aix-en-Provence, which he has painted back to front. Like the reversed notes on the later **Verrazano Narrows,** this is an exercise in forming a conception from visual data. For all of us the forms of letters have to be conceptualised through education so that we can read a variety of scripts. At the same time the practice of writing has grown automatic. The trick of writing

Ladies of Texas 1975

backwards is to separate the mental concept, to alter it and to feed it back to the hand which has to overcome its habits and consciously relearn the new set. Such a painting as **Ladies of Texas** then, is both an event and a test of self.

The device of a white border used on many of the pictures described so far, was abandoned in the 'seventies. **Los Angeles Yellow Pages** has its own typographic mask or border, but in **Piccadilly Circus** the mask is no longer rectilinear but is the quasi-random arrangement of brush strokes through which the image appears. This was a unique device. More consistently, Morley experimented with a three-dimensional mask or framework. It should be pointed out that there had often been an implied three-dimensional framework to the earlier pictures comprising the visual frustrum of a pyramid lying between the aperture in the card and the surface of the picture, but this had been treated as a limit only and was not painted.

Gerald Gaziorwski: Model of a train wreck

Train Wreck 1975

Train Wreck is avowedly an accident. It is a picture of the carriages of a model train, heaped up in a shallow box whose sides appear in the picture, lettered in Chinese, Cyrillic and Japanese scripts: 'catastrophe' and 'train wreck'. The lettering is that of newspapers, the theme is related to that of Warhol's automobile smashes. Morley had been able to paint ships (the genus of the original model in the repressed incident) provided that they were immaculate and that the paint was equally discreet. In order to paint more violently and to paint a violent scene, he had first to displace the event from ship to train.

As a means of painting, Morley had stretched a string grid over the open side of the box. A

friend, Gerald Gaziorwsky, was a collector of models and constructed train wrecks. For Morley, the association of models with catastrophe was a powerful one (as a result perhaps of the cirumstance of the bombing mentioned above). The brush strokes are getting freer, a sign of willingness of the artist to show feeling.

Age of Catastrophe 1976

Age of Catastrophe goes a step nearer the traumatic event. Here the subjects are both ship and aeroplane, but the plane has 'crashed' on the ship. It is not a bomber but a commercial plane in which one might oneself suffer a crash and extinction. The hiddenness of the scene is perhaps referred to by the presence of a U-boat which is, however, paradoxically flying, suspended by threads from two twigs which appear at the top, from which there also hangs a dead bird. At the same time it is floating beneath the sea, that is, it appears beneath the ship. In fact almost every element of the painting can be interpreted or loaded with personal symbolic associations. The same plane, a tin Pan American Airways Constellation (long out of use at the time of painting) appears in **Burial of Catastrophe** in which orange flowers spring up around it like flames.

In these paintings the model has become three-dimensional but not yet real. It is staged in miniature. It is not clear to what degree the toy used as a model had already been demaged since a new development affects these paintings. If one imagines oneself looking through an aperture or grid to paint each section, then, if the procedure is not self-regulating, one may perhaps slightly misalign the eye. If such an 'accident' is accepted and treated literally, then that element will appear out of phase, shifted, on the canvas, a *sdvig*. The dovetailed form of the shifts on the right is due to the use of a diagonal as well as a rectangular grid. The model for **Age of Catastrophe** was a small tableau comprising a reproduction of his own picture, **SS Amsterdam in Front of Rotterdam,** as the background for the models of plane and submarine. A feature of his earlier work had been that the reproduction of one of his pictures was indistinguishable from the original postcard, so that a painting of the reproduction of the original painting should be indistinguishable from the painting. The aim is (near) perfect visual identity. I have already mentioned how this can be destroyed by movement to a point too close to

the picture. A flat image is not normally affected by lateral movement of the eye (by parallax) but, by the device described, Morley has brought this kind of shift to bear even on the painting of a flat model. In this way he destroys the implied two-dimensionality of the image by making it clear that it can suffer from distortion by virtue of its distance relative to the imagined picture plane. By association, he damages both the image and its subject. The work **Teacup** originally demonstrated the method in itself, for the grid and framework which he had used to fix and shift the image was attached to the bottom of the picture when it was first exhibited. The painting shows the inside of the cup looked at directly from above. Shifts of viewpoint distort the perspective of the image in the way in which it is conjectured that Cézanne produced certain characteristic distortions

Verrazano Narrows 1976

The same problem, how to reconcile different viewpoints of the motif on a single picture plane, had been a germinal one for the Cubists and other artists of the early twentieth century. It comes into play not only if the artist rotates the motif but if he or she moves around it. It also comes into play even if the eye remains still, but, in order to survey a wide scene, it rotates, carrying with it an imagined picture plane perpendicular to the line of sight. In the **Teacup** the viewpoint had been fixed within quite narrow limits, but in **Verrazano Narrows** Morley confronted the last problem in an acute form. For it arises most dramatically in the case of a wide landscape or a tall thin object like a tower. The eye has to rotate only on one axis: to pan or to scan (up and down). Here, by taking his stance at the top of the New York World Trade Centre and by looking out over the river's skirting point of Manhattan Island, he gave himself the problem in both dimensions. The result is an expression of vertigo which I think may be brought on because the world seems to rotate at the margins as one moves one eyes down to the ground or up to the sky from a high point. **Verrazano Narrows** is painted in ways, however, which partially 'control' the problem.

The method devised was that Morley would make first a drawing on the site and this would be divided in two parts, one to be painted by Morley himself and one by his assistant, Rick

Britzenhoff. Each worked from the lines of the drawing and also from colour notes which indicated both the colour to be used and formed part of the drawing. Thus they appear in the painting but backwards. The verbal indication, however, was not quite specific enough for the two parts to match as accurately in colour as they do in configuration (drawing). The characteristic gestures of the brush strokes of the two painters are surprisingly similar. The paler left half tends rather more to uniformity and horizontality. The space in the painting is quite primitive – recession is indicated by the diagonal, as in the earlier paintings of ships. There is a hint here of Alfred Wallis, the 'primitive' St. Ives painter whom Morley came to admire. Another, quite different primitive source, is Giotto. His angels from the *Pietà* in the Arena Chapel in Padua are flying over New York.

The technique of reversal (apparently by conceptual transformation rather than by using a mirror) has forced the hand to show. For muscles accustomed to writing forwards, write backwards much more awkwardly, deforming the shapes and tending to revert to the more usual habit. In the archaic script along the lower edge (where Britzenhoff is acknowledged in an old form of abbreviation), the letter 'z' is reversed. So one may conjecture that the lettering in the model was itself reversed so that it would be reversed again and come out correctly.

Nevertheless the most important picture of 1977 was again an overtly political one. Morley went to Berlin through the D.A.A.D. (German Academic Exchange) programme and worked at the Krankenhaus overlooking the Wall. For Morley, the building was aptly named: he became ill not long after and left, but the picture is based on the experience of the Wall. Its title, **The Day of the Locust,** comes from that of Nathaniel West's novel of Hollywood with which it shares violence and theatrical unreality exemplified in the novel's opening scene in which cavalry ride down Wilshire Boulevard. To paint it, Morley set up a tableau comprising, at the back, a poster of his own **Los Angeles Yellow Pages** and, above it, a small reproduction of his earlier **SS Amsterdam in Front of Rotterdam.** In front of this he built the wall, beset by anachronistic soldiers and other little figures who act out a conflict. Others violate the background by being stuck through it. Morley had in mind Artaud's 'Theatre of Cruelty': specifically his description of a production in which the actors were fingers and arms stuck through a curtain. In **The Day of the Locust** a ladder connects the space of the wall with the 'illusion' of Los Angeles and allegorically with the commercial culture listed in the 'Yellow Pages'. The word 'Angeles' above conjures up angels in the sky. I take the anachronism of the fighting figures and the presence of Hollywood-style Red Indians to represent the inappropriate survival of the culture and institutions of hunting and warfare in our society because of the horrifying instruments that we now have for both oppression and annihilation. The picture was painted while

The Day of the Locust 1977

looking through a grid that had been placed some distance in front in order to accommodate the three-dimensional tableau. This allowed the artist to exploit the spatial shifts that could occur relative to the grid, if his eye position changed (or if he looked through the other eye), as may be seen most conspicuously up the left-hand edge of the picture. Using such a device and taking advantage of such accidents presented the artist with another means of transforming the surface.

He learned from what he had done. For the so-called Photo-realist paintings, the plane of the postcard or other printed matter could be divided into sections in a manner identical with that of the canvas. The resulting grid is two-dimensional but the accuracy of the representation of the photographic image is such that the illusion of three dimensions is virtually complete. When the model is three-dimensional, as in the earlier **Age of Catastrophe** as well as **Day of the Locust**, this is no longer possible. The accuracy of the projection depends on the eye of the painter remaining quite still (cf. Dürer's woodcut illustrated above). However, both literally and metaphorically, in terms of the social role allocated to the artist, his eye cannot remain still. By representing the literal case directly through its failure, Morley dramatises the role of the artist in representing the world. The problem of representation is seen to lie in the pyramid between the eye and the canvas and between the eye and the model (that is, what the artist sees) rather than between the image and what is represented (the accuracy of the image). The picture shifts and tends to disintegrate so that the flux and contradiction of the painting can be read as an allegory of the state of the world in which the painter lives.

However, it must be emphasised that the role of such stratagems and even allegories is finally to allow, assist or compel the artist to paint effective pictures. The turbulent character of the paint-work here is both the subject-matter and the vehicle of the painter.

The Ultimate Anxiety is based on a postcard of a painting by Francesco Guardi sent to him from Venice. It is his last picture based on a two-dimensional representation by someone else and breaks a rule that Morley had made for himself in about 1976, to paint only from

models generated by the action of his own hand. Perhaps in this case the affinity of the handling of the Guardi with Morley's own handling made it possible. The extra element in the picture (whose subject-matter, the 'Buccintore' carrying the Doge in his ceremony of wedding the sea, is an analogue of the cruise liners of Morley's past) is the train which cuts across **The Ultimate Anxiety** as if to cross the picture out. This is the only instance among Morley's paintings where the grid is drawn over the picture and remains part of its apparatus. It carries the train in a fashion that resembles both certain floor works by Carl Andre, and closer to the theme, train-tracks themeselves. Related to these, and because of its diagonal slant, the train (taken from a mailorder catalogue of 'Best Products') appears to have crashed on the anachronistic ship.

The Ultimate Anxiety 1978

The evidence of the grid shows that the train was painted on top of the complete ship. One of the few prototypes of this instance, very rare in Morley's work, is the analogous cross painted over **Race Track**. Almost always, superimpositions in his paintings are illusory. They are created in advance in the model, so that the act of painting is the final act. Generally he paints directly, wet on wet, so that there is no underpainting and little alteration. All is revealed.

This process is exemplified in **Day of the Locust III.** It is based on parts of the original picture (itself based on two earlier ones), rearranged. A single dragoon (referring to the troop of cavalry in the opening chapter of West's novel) is inserted in the form of the representation of a modelled and painted figurine. That, in turn, is based on Géricault's well-known composition of a cuirassier. The figure is, however, turned round, so that the side that Géricault did not paint is the one that Morley discloses.

The military theme is taken up again in several works, especially **The Grand Bayonet Charge of the French Legionnaires in the Sahara.** The model is a single toy less than three inches high, drawn and painted over and over again. The additional element (which carries a decypherable message) is that the patterned or regimented distribution of the figures achieves

the result that they all appear to be stabbing one another in the back. Alternatively they can be considered as having been reduced to a decoration, with a wallpaper-like repeat and a colour system based on the contrast of blue and yellow. No other devices are necessary in this relatively simple work. But a mis-match of proportion between the drawing and the painting, like that described in the much earlier **Empire Monarch** is solved not by painting the margin black, but by repeating on it an arbitrary vertical section from the centre left of the picture. This is another form of shift.

In the previous year, 1978, Morley had completed several apparently, more straight-forward works. They were inspired by a visit to Florida and to the Bush Garden Zoo and Park there. The background of these pictures is the green of lush Florida. In one, tiny models of the TV series and film, M.A.S.H. (a grocery-store giveaway) share the space with some ghostly white figures. One of them, representing Morley's doctor, rides on an elephant. The crosses on the operating tent and ambulance in this painting, (called **M.A.S.H.**) though red, were associated in Morley's mind with the cross compositions by the Russian artist, Malevich. So they have been given an additional meaning from the tradition of art.

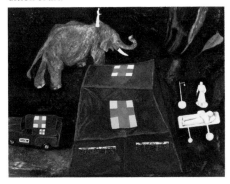

M.A.S.H. 1978

Bush Garden served as an inspiration for **Parrots**, the most direct painting he had done so far. It is based on a single watercolour, (for studies from nature in this medium had frequently become Morley's model) drawn in this Florida location. The colours are complementary, principally red and green but also blue and yellow. Hidden under green paint, as if absorbed by the vegetation, is the outline of the birds' artificial avatar, the jet fighter, but it is hardly visible to disturb the peace and the feast of the senses.

For Morley such a picture approaches the pure pleasure principle. The senses and the

bodily act of painting have reached a condition of harmony but this is not a state that could be long maintained. Pictures that carried or were motivated by emotions of conflict also demanded realisation.

Out Dark Spot is one of them. The title is a variation on Lady Macbeth's 'Out damned spot' and seems to echo other very well-known phrases from Skakespeare's play: 'Is this a dagger which I see before me' and even, 'this my hand will rather the multitudinous seas incarnadine, making the green one red'. The picture is, in any case, mainly green and red, though it again contains the contrasts yellow and blue, added to black and white. There are a number of images in varying perspectives and scales, but they are organised into a rough, over-all symmetry and also, into a dramatic unity. The field of the picture comprises green water in which flamingoes are wading, their bodies appearing as white areas from which the legs run down, like trickles of blood. There are two mangoes hanging in the upper-right-hand corner. Two Red Indians draw broken bows to either side and frame a jagged slit down the centre. At the top of this is a military jet; in the centre, the vignette of a view of a street seen from above, with a street light and part of a tank. At the bottom there is a Nazi flag impaled by a cooking knife.

Out Dark Spot 1978

There can be no doubt that Out Dark Spot is both a working out, or confession, of inner feelings of aggression and an allegory of the gross excess of actual and potential violence. Such violence results from the suppression and transformation of original drives and pleasures by complex and dangerous electro-mechanical and impersonal social systems. It is possible to see in it fetishistic substitutions for vulva, clitoris, phallus and so on. However, I believe that in the end, such readings are no more important to the overall meaning than the small lead Indian from which the two large figures of **Out Dark Spot** were painted. It is easy to see that this figure is painted back and front in the kind of symmetry found in the archers painted by Pollaiuolo in the fifteenth-century *St. Sebastian* in the National Gallery in London. There they have a target, unlike Morley's impotent archers, who aim into the void. Furthermore there is a technical variation, for one of Morley's figures was painted directly onto the canvas

(the frontal view on the right) while the other model was first drawn in pastel and the characteristic marks of that medium are faithfully rendered in oil.

In fact, the element painted first was the view of the pavement and lamp standard in the centre, which, because of its scale and high viewpoint, seems more distant (even dream-like). It is a mannerist space, where the foreground encloses the background. The knowledge of and the ability to see and understand such devices, goes further, I believe, to make apparent the quality of the painting, than the reading of political and psychological references.

An obviously still more complex painting is **Christmas Tree (The Lonely Ranger Lost in the Jungle of Erotic Desires).** The title derives from the comment of a neighbour in Florida who said the picture looked like a Christmas tree. The theme is very plainly psychological. The picture centres on a cowboy, symbol of genitally-dominated male sensuality, armed only with a dildo. His arm is 'accidentally' separated from his shoulder by a parrot's tail so that he/you can disown it. Around him are various phallic emblems (the cobra and the train) and filling the rest of the picture, an image of (partly domesticated) primitive sensuality – the parrots in the forest. Above are the dancing legs of a shop window dummy, cut off at the crutch. You find also magical signs, the red sun and the white moon, the Buddah-given mark and the head of the cobra.

Once more there are traditional devices of painting that structure the sense of beauty or harmony. These are colour complements, (red and green, blue and yellow) and, very difficult to find, the proportion of the Golden Section. Morley has used the latter to generate a diagonal comprising the head of the parrot, upper left, of the cowboy and of the cobra. They are no more (or less) than tactical devices that show the artist's determination to be and to succeed as a painter. A painter can be defined as one who by practising the physical act of painting may change his own, and other people's perception of the world.

Since 1980 Morley has practised two kinds of painting. Both are normally based on watercolours or drawings following his acknowledgement of the importance of these media, as well as print making. Previously he had considered oil (or acrylic) to be the unique public medium by which an artist embodied his experience and

Christmas Tree (The Lonely Ranger Lost in the Jungle of Erotic Desires) 1979

established his reputation. For years before **Verrazano Narrows**, drawing had theoretically not even been part of the preparation for painting, which was an independent act. But it had become progressively the means by which, treated faithfully as a model, gesture could be recreated in the paintings.

Landscape with Horses 1980

Landscape with Bullocks 1981

The 'natural' paintings, **Landscape with Horses, Landscape with Bullocks** and **Till the Cows come Home** are painted in such a way that the quality of watercolour is captured through the manner of handling the oil in which they are painted. This remains so even when there was an intermediate stage of lithography and even when the paint is applied with the fingers and not the brush (**Till the Cows come Home**). The other two (**Landscape with Horses and Landscape with Bullocks**) are immensely enlarged (to the scale of 108x72″) from single watercolours, each about 42x30″. The effect of broad washes and white paper is simulated with generally opaque strokes of the brush, similar in size to those of the model, but smaller in relation to the scale of the large painting.

The simulated and actual brush strokes estab-

lish a morphological similarity between the animals, the landscape and the clouds. The degree of painterly abstraction is increased though the subject remains unequivocal. There is a sense in which Morley paints that which resembles the reflexes of his own painting style, so that a single rhythm engulfs the picture, that of his own body. He may derive a kind of ecstasy from such a sense of unity of the world in mind and body. The three paintings are upright and have no foreground element to distance them perceptively, which reinforces the immediacy and unity. So the sense of being inside the landscape is one that has been caught in the watercolour and is present in the painting.

Camels and Goats is an unusual picture, painted on three joined canvases. In the one on the right, two camels share a single space. A second look reveals that one camel is the same as the other but scaled-down to about one third. In fact, the smaller one was painted from the habit learned in painting the larger, so that its apparent distance is a function, not of perspective, but of scale, of physical movement only. This applies to its outlines, but at close range, one can see that the brush strokes are almost as large in the small camel as in the large. So there is less information per unit of area.

The two other canvases of the triptych depict, respectively, part of a goat (with the head of another) and the same goat with another on a smaller scale. The space, naturally, is disjointed. The smaller goats are further away, but cannot be occupying the same space. They are in sharper focus and seem to require to be seen in greater close-up. Such a fragmentation of space is normally painted by Morley within the picture, as for example, in **The Grand Bayonet Charge of the Legionnaires**. **Camels and Goats** like **Verrazano Narrows** the **The Ultimate Anxiety** are rare exceptions.

Camels and Goats 1980

All the animals in **Camels and Goats** were originally drawn at Cap Ferrat in southern France. The canvas of camels was a complete picture as was the smaller one of goats. The large goat was an unfinished, larger picture which had originally corresponded in composition to the small goats and was painted earlier from the same drawing. It was cut down when it 'failed'. At this date the link between subject and the consciously lived movements of the painting

arm, have become so close that it may not be possible for Morley to paint a given motif in any arbitrary scale – there will have to be a consonance between the original object, the marks of the watercolour model and those of the finished painting. They are easy to see in the three parts of this painting and extend to such elementary analogies as the humps of the camel and the hills beyond. There is also a common-sense of animality to the creatures represented. They have not been loaded with too many projected human values, they are smelly and awkward. But the three pictures were, in fact, put together some time after they were painted, on the advice of Peter Hawkins.

Macaws, Bengals, with Mullet 1982

Macaws, Bengals, with Mullet shares with **The Palms of Vai**, a composition divided horizontally, an integral psycho-sexual iconography and a fully liberated painterliness. **Macaws, Bengals, with Mullet** presents itself as an altar piece dedicated to the senses. At the lowest level tightly-packed fishes swim in an ocean of feeling. They brush against one another and are beings entirely comprised in their phallic form. Above, the muscular tigers relax, confident in their own potency. In the top half, parrots sit in a phallic tree, an ancient symbol of man's fertility. The birds themselves seem to represent an aerial rather than an earthly or oceanic sexuality, but both in their overall shape and in their tails they are again phallic; the allusion to Freud's analysis of Leonardo's dream seems indirect. The message in the picture cannot of course be written out in words since the action of painting has become both the allegorical and physical product of comprehensive sensuality. At the same time the iconography and other in the composition arise from and represent directly the layered complexity of the human psyche.

In this final splendid work, perhaps more completely than any that had gone before, the technical and compositional devices are transcended in a painterly prophetic utterance.

Belly
1973

Empire Monarch
1965

Cristoforo Colombo
1965

United States with N.Y. Skyline
1965

SS Amsterdam in Front of Rotterdam
1966

On Deck
1966

Ship's Dinner Party
1966

Marine Sergeant at Valley Forge
1968

Vermeer, Portrait of the Artist in his Studio
1968

Rhine Chateau
1969

south africa

Greyville Race Course – Durban, South Africa

Race Track
1970

Kodak Castle
1971

Los Angeles Yellow Pages
1971

School of Athens
1972

Piccadilly Circus
1973

New York City Postcard Fold-Out
1973

Room at Chelsea
1972

Untitled Souvenirs, Europe
1973

SS France
1974

Miami Postcard Fold-Out
1973

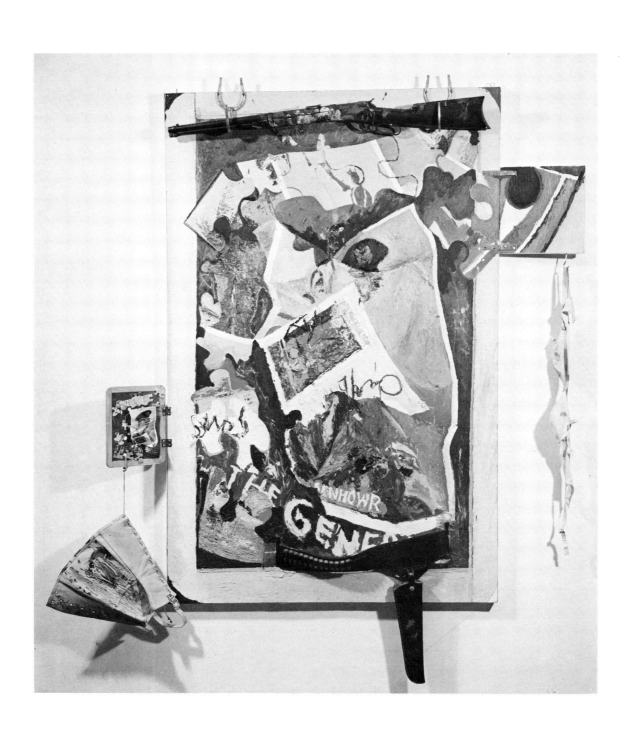

The General
1974

Main Beach, Easthampton
1975

Train Wreck
1975

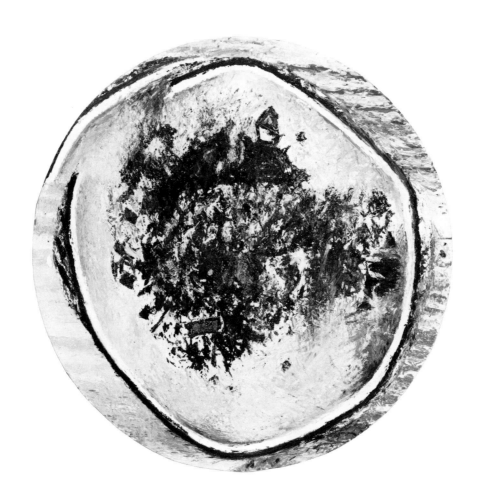

Teacup
1975

Ladies of Texas
1975

Marine Pastoral
1976

Verrazano Narrows
1976

Peripatetic Cross
1976

A Passion for the Funeral of Vincent van Gogh
1975

Age of Catastrophe
1976

Little Corner of Plane-Ship Catastrophe and Central Park
1976

Burial of Catastrophe
1976

The Ultimate Anxiety
1978

The Day of the Locust
1977

Day of the Locust III
1977

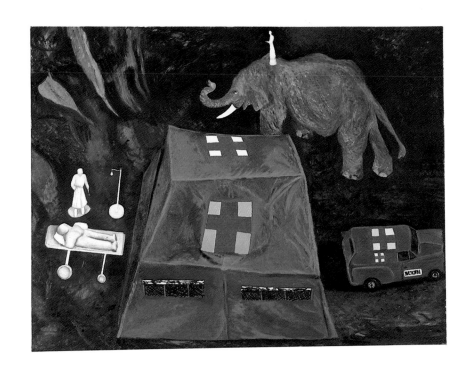

M.A.S.H.
1978

Out Dark Spot
1978

Parrots
1978

Christmas Tree – The Lonely Ranger Lost in the Jungle of Erotic Desires
1979

The Grand Bayonet Charge of the Legionnaires in the Sahara
1979

Camels and Goats
1980

Landscape with Horses
1980

Landscape with Bullocks
1981

La Plage
1980

Underneath the Lemon Tree
1981

Arizonac
1981

Macaws, Bengals, with Mullet
1982

Untitled
1982

Till the Cows Come Home

1981

The Palms of Vai
1982

**Alexander Greeting A.B. Seaman Ulysses MA Evans Jr
at the Foot of the Peanigh**
1982

Catalogue

Dimensions are given first in inches and then in centimetres, height first.
Some paintings will not be available for all showings on the tour.

Empire Monarch
1965
Acrylic on canvas
18x36 (45.8x91.5)
Larry and Cindy Meeker,
Kansas City, Kansas

Cristoforo Colombo
1965
Acrylic on canvas
14x20 (35.5x51)
Jean Christophe Castelli,
New York

United States with N.Y. Skyline
1965
Acrylic on canvas
45³/₈x59³/₈ (115.5x151)
Mr and Mrs Morton Neumann,
Chicago

SS Amsterdam in Front of Rotterdam
1966
Acrylic on canvas
62x84 (157.5x213.5)
Doris and Charles Saatchi,
London

Cristoforo Colombo
1966
Acrylic on canvas
45x60 (114.5x152.5)
Paul and Camille Oliver-Hoffmann,
Charlottesville, Virginia

On Deck
1966
Acrylic on canvas
83³/₄x63³/₄ (212.8x162)
Metropolitan Museum of Art, New York
Gift of Mr and Mrs S. Brooks Barron

Ship's Dinner Party
1966
Acrylic on canvas
82¹/₂x63 (210x160)
Museum van Hedendaagse Kunst,
Utrecht

Marine Sergeant at Valley Forge
1968
Acrylic on canvas
60x50 (152.5x127)
Private collection,
Paris

**Vermeer, Portrait of the Artist
in his Studio**
1968
Acrylic on canvas
105x87 (266.5x221)
Private collection,
Sweden

Castle with Sailboats
1969
Acrylic on canvas
32x46 (81.5x117)
Bo Alveryd,
Kävlinge, Sweden

Rhine Chateau
1969
Acrylic on canvas
28¹/₂x37 (72.5x94)
Private collection,
Paris

Race Track
1970
67x86³/₄ (170x220)
Acrylic with encaustic on canvas
Ludwig Collection,
Neue Galerie, Aachen

Buckingham Palace with First Prize
1970
Acrylic with encaustic on canvas
with objects attached
72x98 (203x249)
Bo Alveryd,
Kävlinge, Sweden

Los Angeles Yellow Pages
1971
Acrylic and encaustic on canvas
84x72 (233x203)
Louisiana Museum of Modern Art,
Humlebaek, Denmark

Kodak Castle
1971
Oil on gesso board
36x48 (91.5x122)
Munson-Williams-Proctor Institute,
Utica, New York

At a First Station, Vietnam
1971
Acrylic and encaustic on canvas
72x106 (183x269)
Bo Alveryd,
Kävlinge, Sweden

School of Athens
1972
Oil and acrylic on canvas
67x94¹/₂ (170x240)
Doris and Charles Saatchi,
London

Room at Chelsea
1972
Oil on canvas, with key
48x36 (122x91.5)
Xavier Fourcade Inc, New York

Untitled Souvenirs, Europe
1973
Oil on canvas
96¹/₄x68¹/₄ (244.5x173.3)
Bo Alveryd,
Kävlinge, Sweden

Belly
1973
Oil on canvas
37¹/₂x36¹/₄ (95x97)
Magnus Bromander,
Göteborg

Piccadilly Circus
1973
Oil on canvas
72x108 (183x274.5)
Private collection,
Sweden

The General
1974
Oil and mixed media on canvas
with objects attached
60x40 (152.5x101.5)
Xavier Fourcade Inc,
New York

SS France
1974
Oil and mixed media on canvas
with objects attached
72x64 (183x162.5)
Doris and Charles Saatchi,
London

Ladies of Texas
1975
Oil on canvas
42x30 (106.5x76)
Xavier Fourcade Inc,
New York

Main Beach, Easthampton
1975
Oil and encaustic on canvas
31¹/₂x47¹/₂ (80x120.5) oval
Larry and Cindy Meeker,
Kansas City, Kansas

Train Wreck
1975
Oil on canvas
60x96 (152.5x244)
Ludwig Stiftung – Museum Moderner Kunst,
Vienna

Age of Catastrophe
1976
Oil on canvas
60x96 (152.5x244)
Doris and Charles Saatchi,
London

Verrazano Narrows
1976
Oil on canvas
59x78³/₄ (150x200)
Janne and Carl Christian Aegidius,
Paris

Marine Pastoral
1976
Oil on canvas with mixed media collage
31x46 (78.7x116.8)
Private collection,
New York

Chateau II
1976
Oil on canvas
80x96 (203.2x244)
Klaus and Anneliese Wolf, Essen

Little Corner of Plane-Ship Catastrophe and Central Park
1976
Oil on canvas
30x36 (76x91.5)
Sydney and Frances Lewis,
Richmond, Virginia

Burial of Catastrophe
1976
Oil on canvas
18 (45.8) (diameter)
Private collection,
Essen

The Day of the Locust
1977
Oil on canvas
72x60 (183x152.5)
Private collection,
Munich

M.A.S.H.
1978
Oil on canvas
36x48 (91.5x122)
Museum of Contemporary Art, Chicago
(National Endowment for the Arts Museum
Matching Purchase Plan,
The Collectors Group,
The Men's Council and the Women's Board)

The Ultimate Anxiety
1978
Oil on canvas
72⁵/₈x98³/₄ (185.3x250.8)
Nancy Hoffman,
New York

Out Dark Spot
1978
Oil on canvas
72⁵/₈x98³/₄ (185.3x250.8)
Jacqueline and Julian Schnabel,
New York

Parrots
1978
Oil on canvas
47x58¹/₂ (119.5x148.5)
Robert Miller Gallery,
New York

Parrots
1978
Oil on canvas
23³/₄x30 (59.8x76)
Jack H. Klein,
New York

**Christmas Tree –
The Lonely Ranger Lost in the Jungle
of Erotic Desires**
1979
Oil on canvas
72x108 (183x274.5)
Stanley J. Seeger,
Sutton Place, Guildford, England

**The Grand Bayonet Charge
of the Legionnaires in the Sahara**
1979
Oil on canvas
72x108 (183x274.5)
Sydney and Frances Lewis,
Richmond, Virginia

Day of the Locust III
1979
Oil on canvas
48x48 (122x122)
Bud Bernstein,
Birmingham, Michigan,
courtesy Susanne Hilberry Gallery

Camels and Goats
1980
Oil on canvas
66¹/₂x100 (169x254)
Doris and Charles Saatchi,
London

Landscape with Horses
1980
Oil on canvas
108x72 (274.5x183)
Mr and Mrs Richard C. Hedreen,
Seattle, Washington

La Plage
1980
Oil on canvas
72x98³/₄ (183x250.8)
Martin Z. Margulies,
Coconut Grove, Florida

Landscape with Bullocks
1981
Oil on canvas
108x72 (274.5x183)
Sydney and Frances Lewis,
Richmond, Virginia

Underneath the Lemon Tree
1981
Oil on canvas
57x75 (145x190.5)
Sydney and Frances Lewis,
Richmond, Virginia

Till the Cows Come Home
1981
Oil on canvas
50x38 (127x96.5)
Robert B. Shapiro,
Skokie, Illinois

Arizonac
1981
Oil on canvas
80x105 (203x266.5)
Doris and Charles Saatchi,
London

Macaws, Bengals, with Mullet
1982
Oil on canvas
120x80 (305x203)
Doris and Charles Saatchi,
London

The Palms of Vai
1982
Oil on canvas
50x40 (127x101.5)
Xavier Fourcade Inc,
New York

**Alexander Greeting
AB Seaman Ulysses MA Evans Jr
at the Foot of the Peanigh**
1982
Oil on canvas
36x42 (91.5x106.5)
Xavier Fourcade Inc,
New York

Untitled
1982
Oil on canvas
80x100 (203x254)
Xavier Fourcade Inc,
New York

Exhibitions and Bibliography

Compiled by Hilary Gresty

One-Person Exhibitions

1964:
October-November: Kornblee Gallery,
New York

1967:
February: Kornblee Gallery, New York

1969:
February-March: Kornblee Gallery,
New York

1972:
September-October: Galerie de Gestlo,
Hamburg
October-November: Galerie Art in Progress,
Zurich

1973:
October: Stefanotty Gallery, New York

1974:
April: Galerie M.E. Thelen, Cologne
August: Stefanotty Gallery, New York
November-December: Galerie Gerald Piltzer,
Paris

1976:
October: The Clocktower, Institute for Art and
Urban Resources, New York (catalogue)

1977:
July-August: Galerie Jöllenbeck, Cologne
October-November: Galerie Jurka, Amsterdam

1979:
April-May: Nancy Hoffman Gallery,
New York
October-November: Susanne Hilberry Gallery,
Birmingham, Michigan

1980:
January-March: Matrix 54, Wadsworth
Atheneum, Hartford, Connecticut
(catalogue)

1981:
April-May: Xavier Fourcade Inc, New York

1981-82:
November-January: Akron Art Institute,
Akron, Ohio

1982:
December: Xavier Fourcade Inc, New York

Note

An asterisk indicates that the catalogue or periodical was not available for examination by the compiler and information is therefore derived from secondary sources. Some general articles with illustrations of work by Malcolm Morley, but no text reference, have been excluded. Reviews of group exhibitions in which work by Morley was shown have only been included where there is a mention of Morley in the text or illustrations.

Group Exhibitions

1955:
Young Contemporaries, London (as M.J. Evans)

1966:
The Photographic Image, Solomon
R. Guggenheim Museum, New York
(catalogue)
Sound, Light and Silence, Nelson Gallery,
Atkins Museum, Kansas City (catalogue)

1967:
**Personal Preference: Paintings and Sculpture
from the Collection of Mr & Mrs S. Brooks
Barron*,** University Art Gallery,
Oakland University, New York
Sao Paulo 9 Biennal: **Environment U.S.A.
1957-1967** (catalogue)

1968:
Patriotic Images in American Art*, American
Federation of Arts
Realism Now, Vassar College Art Gallery,
Poughkeepsie, New York (catalogue)
Preview 1968, Austin Arts Center, Trinity
College, Hartford, Connecticut (catalogue)

1969:
Aspects of New Realism, Milwaukee Art
Center, Wisconsin; travelled to
Contemporary Arts Museum, Houston and
Akron Art Institute (catalogue)
Pop Art, Hayward Gallery, London (catalogue)
**Biennial Exhibition of Contemporary
American Painting and Sculpture,**
Krannert Art Museum, University of
Illinois, Champaign (catalogue)

1969-70:
Paintings from the Photo, Riverside Museum,
New York (catalogue)

1970:
Directions 70, Part II: The Cool Realists*,
Jack Glenn Gallery, Corona Del May,
California
Wirklicher als Wirklich, Galerie M.E. Thelen,
Cologne
22 Realists, Whitney Museum of American
Art, New York (catalogue)
American Art Since 1960, The Art
Museum, Princeton University, N.J.
(catalogue)
Kunst um 1970, Neue Galerie der Stadt
Aachen (catalogue)

1971:
Each in His Own Way, The Museum of
Science and Industry, Chicago (catalogue)
**Kunst des 20 Jahrhunderts, (Freie Berufe
Sammeln)** Städtische Kunsthalle,
Düsseldorf (catalogue)
Shape of Realism*, Deson Zaks Gallery,
Chicago
Neue Amerikanische Realisten*,
Galerie de Gestlo, Hamburg
Radical Realism, Museum of Contemporary
Art, Chicago (catalogue)

1972:
Colossal Scale, Sidney Janis Gallery,
New York (catalogue)
**Annual Exhibition of Contemporary American
Painting,** Whitney Museum of American
Art, New York (catalogue)
Sharp Focus Realism, Sidney Janis Gallery,
New York (catalogue)
Documenta 5, Kassel (catalogue)
Documenta und Nodocumenta Realists*,
Galerie de Gestlo, Hamburg (catalogue)
Art for McGovern*, New York
Gallery as Studio*, University Art Gallery,
State University of New York at
Stony Brook

1972-73:
Amerikanischer Fotorealismus,
Württembergischer Kunstverein, Stuttgart;
travelled to: Frankfurt Kunstverein and
Kunst und Museumverein, Wuppertal until
1973 (catalogue)

1973:
**Ein Grosse Jahrzehnt Amerikanischer
Kunst: Sammlung Ludwig Köln/Aachen*,**
Kunstmuseum, Lucerne (catalogue)
**Image, Reality and Superreality: Prints
Bought for the Arts Council Collection
by Edward Lucie-Smith 1972-3,**
Arts Council, London; touring exhibition
(catalogue)
**Werkelijkheid is Meervoud: Realisme uit de
Verzameling Ludwig, Neue Galerie Aken*,**
Groningen, Museum voor Stadt en Lande
(catalogue)
Time Magazine Building*, New York
Zeichnungen Sommer 1973, Galerie
M.E. Thelen, Cologne (catalogue)
The Super-Realist Vision, De Cordova and
Dana Park Museum, Lincoln,
Massachusetts (catalogue)
American Sharp Focus Realism*:
Galleri Löwenadler, Stockholm
American Art: Third Quarter Century,
Seattle Art Museum (catalogue)
Amerikanska Realism*, Galleri Ostergren,
Malmö (catalogue)
Amerikanska Superrealister*, Lunds
Konsthall, Galleri Fabian Carlsson,
Göteborg*
**Photo-Realism: Paintings, Sculpture and
Prints from the Ludwig Collection and
others,** Serpentine Gallery, London
(catalogue)
**Ekstrem Realisme: Vaerker fra Neue Galerie
der Stadt Aachen,** Louisiana Museum of
Modern Art, Humlebaek (catalogue in
Louisiana Revy, February, 13 årg., nr.3,
pp.39-40)
Grands Maîtres Hyperréalistes Americains,
Galerie des 4 Mouvements, Paris and
travelled to International Art Fair, Basel
(catalogue)
Mit Kamera, Pinsel und Spritzpistole,
Ruhrfestspiele Recklinghausen, Städtische
Kunsthalle, Recklinghausen

Photo Realism 1973: The Stuart M. Speiser Collection, Louis K. Meisel Gallery, New York; travelled to: Herbert F. Johnson Museum of Fine Art, Ithaca; Memorial Art Gallery, University of Rochester; and throughout the United States until 1978 (catalogue)

1973-74:

Kunst nach Wirklichkeit: ein neuer Realismus in Amerika und in Europa*, Hannover Kunstverein (catalogue)

Hyperréalisme*, Galerie Isy Brachot, Brussels (catalogue)

1974:

Aachen International 70-74, Festival Exhibition, Royal Scottish Academy, Edinburgh (catalogue)

Art Conceptuel et Hyperréaliste: Collection Ludwig, Neue Galerie Aix-la-Chapelle*, Musée d'Art Moderne de la Ville de Paris, ARC (catalogue)

Dealers Choice/Choice Dealers*, The New York Cultural Center Annex, New York

Hyperréalistes Americains: Réalistes Européens, Centre National d'Art Contemporain, Paris (catalogue)

Kunst bleibt Kunst: Projekt '74, Kunsthalle Cologne (catalogue)

Kijken naar de Werkelijkheid: Amerikaanse Hyperrealisten, Europese Realisten, Museum Boymans-van Beuningen, Rotterdam (catalogue)

25 Years of Janis, Sidney Janis Gallery, New York (catalogue)

1974-75:

Imagist Realism*, Norton Gallery and School of Art, West Palm Beach, Florida; travelled to: Merriewold West, Far Hills, New Jersey (catalogue)

1975:

Portrait Painting 1970-1975, Allan Frumkin Gallery, New York

Watercolours and Drawings: American Realists*, Louis K. Meisel, New York (catalogue)

1976:

Gerald Laing and Malcolm Morley, Max Hutchinson Gallery, New York.

American Family Portraits*, Philadelphia Museum of Art

New York: Down Town Manhattan: Soho, Akademie der Kunst, Berlin, and Berliner Festwochen (catalogue)

New York in Europa: Amerikanische Kunst aus Europäischen Sammlungen, Nationalgalerie Berlin (catalogue in **Amerikanische Kunst von 1945 bis Heute,** Dieter Honisch and J.C. Jensen, Cologne: DuMont, 1976, pp. 322-328)

Soho*, Louisiana Museum of Modern Art, Humlebaek (catalogue)

1977:

British Painting 1952-1977, Royal Academy of Arts, London (catalogue)

Documenta 6, Kassel (catalogue)

Documenta 6 Künstler, Galerie de Gestlo, Hamburg

Malerei und Photographie im Dialog von 1840 bis Heute, Kunsthaus, Zurich (catalogue)

Second Biennal, works on paper, Louis K. Meisel Gallery, New York

Illusion and Reality, Australian National Gallery, Canberra; travelled to: Western Australian Art Gallery, Perth: Queensland Art Gallery, Brisbane; Art Gallery of New South Wales, Sydney; Art Gallery of South Australia, Adelaide; National Gallery of Victoria, Melbourne, and Tasmanian Museum & Art Gallery, Hobart (catalogue)

1978:

Art about Art, Whitney Museum of American Art, New York; travelled to: North Carolina Museum of Art, Raleigh; Frederick S. Wight Art Gallery, University of California, Los Angeles and Portland Art Museum (catalogue)

Hallwalls*, Buffalo, New York

Landscape/Cityscape*, Brainerd Hall Art Gallery, State University College, Potsdam, New York (catalogue)

Cityscape: 78*, Oklahoma Art Center (catalogue)

Art for Collectors*, The Toledo Museum of Art, Ohio

Artists look at Art, Helen Foresman Spencer Museum of Art, University of Kansas, Lawrence, Kansas (catalogue)

1978-79:

Things Seen, Sheldon Memorial Art Gallery, University of Nebraska, Lincoln and travelled throughout United States (catalogue)

1979:

Biff Elrod, Rafael Ferrer, Malcolm Morley, Joseph Raffael: Recent Works on Paper*, Nancy Hoffman Gallery, New York,

(Group show with works by Malcolm Morley and other artists)*. Edward Thorp Gallery, New York

1980:

Lynda Benglis, Ron Gordon and Malcolm Morley*, Texas Gallery, Houston

Malcolm Morley, Charlotte Moorman, Al Hansen: current work*, Hansen Galleries, New York

Janet Fish, Georgia O'Keefe, Robert Zakanitch, Malcolm Morley: group exhibition*, Robert Miller Gallery, New York

Elizabeth Murray, Jacques Lipchitz, Malcolm Morley, Alex Katz, Joel Shapiro, Susanne Hilberry Gallery, Birmingham, Michigan

One Major New York Each, Xavier Fourcade Inc, New York

Figuration, University Art Museum, Santa Barbara, California (catalogue)

1980-81:

A Penthouse Aviary*, Museum of Modern Art, New York (catalogue)

American Drawings in Black and White 1970-1980, Brooklyn Museum, New York (catalogue)

1981:

A New Spirit in Painting, Royal Academy of Arts, London (catalogue)

Contemporary American Realism since 1960, Pennsylvania Academy of the Fine Arts, Philadelphia (catalogue)

Westkunst: Zeitgenössische Kunst seit 1939, Cologne (catalogue)

Drawings: Group Exhibition, Sperone Westwater Fischer, New York

Painters' Painters, Siegel Contemporary Art, New York

The Image in American Painting and Sculpture 1950-1980, Akron Art Institute, Akron, Ohio (catalogue)

1981-82:

Super Realism from the Morton G. Neumann Family Collection, Kalamazoo Institute of Arts, Michigan; travelled to: The New Art Center, South Bend; Indiana, Springfield Art Museum, Missouri; Dartmouth College Museum, Hanover, New Hampshire; De Cordova and Dana Museum and Park; Lincoln and Des Moines Art Center, Iowa (catalogue)

1982:

Mitchell, Morley, Rockburne: New Prints and Works on Paper, Xavier Fourcade Inc, New York

Landscapes, Robert Miller Gallery, New York

Painting and Sculpture Today 1982, Indianapolis Museum of Art (catalogue)

Issues: New Allegory 1, Institute of Contemporary Arts, Boston (catalogue)

Thirty Painters: Given and Promised, Metropolitan Museum of Art, New York

The Expressionist Image from Pollock to Today, Sidney Janis Gallery, New York

Zeitgeist, Martin-Gropius-Bau, Berlin

Artist's Statements and Interviews

Morley, Malcolm: **Sao Paulo 9: Environment USA 1957-1967,** p.88; reprinted in *Pop Art Redefined* by John Russell and Suzi Gablik, p.95

Kertess, Klaus: 'Malcolm Morley Talking about Seeing', *Artforum,* vol.18, no.10, Summer 1980, pp.48-51, front cover

Levine, Les: 'Dialogue: Malcolm Morley', *Cover,* vol.1, no.3, Spring/Summer 1980, pp.28-31

Books

1969:
Russell, John and Gablik, Suzi: *Pop Art
Redefined,* New York: Praeger; London:
Thames and Hudson

1970:
Compton, Michael: *Pop Art,* London: Hamlyn

1971:
Calas, Nicolas and Elena: *Icons and Images of
the Sixties,* New York: Dutton

1972:
Hunter, Sam: *American Art of the 20th Century,*
New York: Abrams
Kultermann, Udo: *New Realism,* London:
Matthews Miller Dunbar; New York:
New York Graphic Society, (transl. from
German ed. published Tübingen, 1971)

1973:
Sager, Peter: *Neue Formen des Realismus,*
Cologne: Dumont Schauberg

1975:
Battcock, Gregory: *Super Realism: a Critical
Anthology,* New York: Dutton
Chase, Linda: Hyperrealism, London:
Academy (transl. from French ed. published
Paris, 1973)
Walker, John A.: Art Since Pop, London:
Thames and Hudson

1977:
Becker, Wolfgang: *Der Ausgestellte Künstler
Museum Kunst seit 45,* Aachen: Neue
Galerie Sammlung Ludwig. 2 vols.
(Essay: 'The Picture as a Reproduction of a
Reproduction', vol.1, n.p.)
Kultermann, Udo: *The New Painting,* rev. ed.,
Boulder (Colo.): Westview Press,
(transl. from German ed. published
Tübingen, 1976)
Battcock, Gregory: *Why Art? Casual Notes on
the Aesthetics of the Immediate Past,*
New York: Dutton

1979:
Lucie-Smith, Edward: *Super Realism,* Oxford:
Phaidon

1980:
Meisel, Louis K.: *Photorealism,* New York:
Abrams
Lindey, Christine: *Superrealist Painting and
Sculpture,* London: Orbis

Periodical Articles

1964:
Johnston, Jill: 'Reviews and Previews: New
Names This Month', *Art News,* October,
vol.63, no.6, p.16 (review of Kornblee
Gallery exhibition)

1965:
Ashton, Dore: 'New York Commentary',
Studio International, January, vol.169,
no.861, p.25 (review of Kornblee Gallery
exhibition)

1966:
Pincus-Witten; Robert; 'New York', *Artforum,*
March, vol.4, no.7, p.47
(review of Guggenheim exhibition)

1967:
Pincus-Witten: 'Sound Light and Silence in
Kansas City', *Artforum,* January, vol.5,
no.5, pp.51-52 (review of Nelson Gallery
exhibition)
Alloway, Lawrence: 'The Paintings of Malcolm
Morley', *Art and Artists,* February, vol.1,
no.11, pp.16-19
Waldman, Diane: 'Review and Preview',
Art News, February, vol.65, no.10, p.17
(review of Kornblee Gallery exhibition)
Tuten, Frederic: 'In the Galleries',
Arts Magazine, March, vol.41, no.5, p.59
(review of Kornblee Gallery exhibition)
Glueck, Grace: 'New York Gallery Notes:
Color it Unspectacular', *Art in America,*
March/April, vol.55, no.2, pp.102-108
Alloway, Lawrence: 'Art as Likeness (Post Pop
Art)', *Arts Magazine,* May, vol.41, no.7,
pp.34-39

1968:
Alloway, Lawrence: 'Morley Paints a Picture',
Art News, Summer, vol.67, no.4, pp.42-44,
69-71
'Realer than Real', *Time,* 16 August, pp.44-45
Constable, Rosalind: 'Style of the Year:
the Inhumanists',* *New York Magazine,*
16 December, vol.1, no.37, p.44-50

1969:
Tillim, Sidney: 'The Reception of Figurative
Art', *Artforum,* February, vol.7, no.6,
pp.30-33
Dali, Salvador: 'De Kooning's 300,000,000th
Birthday', *Art News,* April, vol.68, no.2,
pp.57, 62-63
Mellow, James R.: 'New York Letter':
Exhibition at Kornblee Gallery, *Art
International,* April, vol.13, no.4, p.37
Levin, Kim: 'Reviews and Previews', *Art News,*
April vol.68, no.2, pp.19-20, 57
(review of Kornblee Gallery exhibition)
Simon, Rita: 'In the Galleries', *Arts Magazine,*
April, vol.43, no.6, p.61 (review of
Kornblee Gallery exhibition)
Pomeroy, Ralph: 'New York: Super-Real is
Back in Town', *Art and Artists,* April, vol.4,
no.2, p.26 (review of Kornblee Gallery
exhibition)
'Super Realism; Hand Painted Copies of
Posters and Calendars', *Life,* 27 June,
vol.66, no.25, pp.44-48

Daley, Janet: 'Pop Vulgarism; *Art and Artists,*
July, vol.4, no.4, pp.44-45
Russell, John: 'Pop Reappraised',
Art in America, July/August, vol.57, no.4,
pp.78-89
Frankenstein, Alfred: 'The High Pitch of New
Realism'*, *San Francisco Sunday
Examiner and Chronicle,* 17 August,
pp.29-30
'Work in Progress', *Esquire,* December, p.210
Alloway, Lawrence: 'Art', *The Nation,*
December, vol.209, no.23, pp.741-742
(review of *Paintings from the Photo*)

1969/70:
Nemser, Cindy: 'In the Museums: Paintings
From the Photo', *Arts Magazine,*
December/January, vol.44, no.3, p.56
(review of *Paintings from the Photo*)

1970:
Atkinson, Tracy, and Taylor, John Lloyd:
'Likenesses', *Art and Artists,* February,
vol.4, no.11, pp.16-21 and front cover
Ratcliff, Carter: 'New York', *Art International,*
April, vol.14, no.4, pp.67-68 (review of *22
Realists* exhibition)
Ratcliff, Carter: 'New York', *Art International,*
March, vol.14, no.3, pp.67-69
(review of *Paintings from the Photo*)
Alloway, Lawrence: 'Notes on Realism', *Arts
Magazine,* April, vol.44, no.6, pp.26-29
(review of *22 Realists* exhibition)
Lord, Barry: 'The Eleven O'Clock News in
Color', *Arts Canada,* June, vol.27, no.3,
pp.4-29

1971:
Dreyfuss, Jane: 'Kodachrome II'*,
Modern Photography, February, pp.62-63
Marandel, J. Patrice: 'Deductive Image:
Notes on Some Figurative Painters',
Art International, September, vol.15, no.7,
pp.58-61 (review of *22 Realists* exhibition)
Sager, Peter: 'Neue Formen des Realismus',
Magazin Kunst, 11 Jahr., Nr.44,
pp.2507-2545

1972:
Pozzi, Lucio: 'Super Realisti USA'*,
Bolaffiarte, March, no.18, pp.54-63
Ashton, Dore: 'New York Commentary:
Realism Again', *Studio International,*
March, vol.183, no.192, pp.126-27
(review of exhibition at Sidney Janis
Gallery)
Hickey, David: 'Sharp Focus Realism at Janis',
Art in America, March/April, vol.60, no.2,
pp.116-18 (review)
Alloway, Lawrence: 'Art', *The Nation,* 5 June,
vol.214, no.23, pp.733-34
Kurtz, B.: 'Documenta 5: A Critical Preview',
Arts Magazine, Summer, vol.46, no.8,
pp.30-37
Seitz, W.C.: 'Real and the Artificial: Painting of
the New Environment', *Art in America,*
November/December, vol.60, no.6,
pp.58-72

Weichardt, Jürgen: 'Neue Landschaft', *Magazin Kunst,* 12 Jahr., Nr.45, p.2663, 2665

1973:
Levin, Kim: 'Malcolm Morley: Post Style Illusionism', *Arts Magazine,* February, vol.47, no.4, pp.60-63
Levin, Kim: 'The Newest Realism: a Synthetic Slice of Life', *Opus International,* June, no.44/45, pp.28-37
Perreault, John: 'Airplane Art in a Headwind', *The Village Voice,* 4 October, p.24 (review of Louis K. Meisel Gallery exhibition)
Mellow, James R.: 'Malcolm Morley', *New York Times,* 10 October (review of Stefanotty Gallery exhibition)
Perreault, John: 'Postcards and a Plastic Rose', *The Village Voice,* 25 October, p.41 (review of Stefanotty Gallery exhibition)
Becker, Wolfgang: 'Het Nieuwe Realisme?', *Museumjournaal,* October serie 18, no.5, pp.210-13
Frank, Peter: 'Stefanotty Gallery, New York', *Art News,* November, vol.72, no.9, pp.100-101
Bell, Jane: 'Malcolm Morley', *Arts Magazine,* December, vol.48, no.3, p.74 (review of Stefanotty Gallery exhibition)

1974:
Slattery, William: 'A Free Wheeling Artist Talks Back', *New York Post,* 28 January 1974, p.36 (review of New York Cultural Center exhibition)
Gassiot-Talabot, G.: 'Le Choc des "Réalismes"', *XXe Siècle,* June, 26 année, no.42, pp.25-32.
Loring, J.: 'Plastic Logic of Realism', *Arts Magazine,* October, vol.48, no.2, p.48-49
Olson, Roberta J.M.: 'Malcolm Morley; *Arts Magazine,* October, vol.49, no.2, p.69 (review of Stefanotty Gallery exhibition)

1975:
Ellenzweig, Ellen: 'Portrait Painting 1970-1975', *Arts Magazine,* March, vol.49, no.7, pp.13-14 (review of Allan Frumkin Gallery exhibition)
Battcock, Gregory: 'New York Developments', *Art and Artists,* February, vol.9, no.11, p.4
Moser, Charlotte: 'Malcolm Morley: Visiting University of Houston Artist, now Portraying 'Romantic Anarchy'*, *Houston Chronicle,* 7 April
Lucie-Smith, Edward: 'The Neutral Style', *Art and Artists,* August, vol.10, no.5, pp.6-15 and front cover

1976:
Patton, Phil: 'Super Realism: A Critical Anthology', *Artforum,* January, vol.4, no.5, pp.52-56 (book review)
Variations sur les Tableaux Actuels'*, *Connaissance des Arts,* March, vol.289, p.112

Kipphoff, Petra: 'Malcolm Morley'*, *Architektur und Wohnen,* April
Chase, Linda: 'Photo-Realism: Post Modernist Illusionism', *Art International,* March/April, vol.20, no.3/4, pp.14-27
Levin, Kim: 'Malcolm Morley', *Arts Magazine,* June, vol.50, no.10, p.11
Russell, John: 'Two Contemporary Realists', *New York Times,* Arts and Leisure Section, 24 October, p.29 (review of Clocktower exhibition)
Rubinfein, Leo: 'Malcolm Morley', *Artforum,* December, vol.15, no.4, pp.63-67 (review of Clocktower exhibition)
Alloway, Lawrence: 'Malcolm Morley', *Unmuzzled Ox,* vol.4, no.2, pp.46-55

1977:
Lubell, Ellen: 'Gerald Laing/Malcolm Morley', *Art Magazine,* February, vol.51, no.6, p.34 (review of Max Hutchinson exhibition)
Kultermann, Udo: 'Vermeer: Versions Modernes'*, *Connaissance des Arts,* April, no.302, pp.94-101
Micha, R.: 'Kassel Documenta 6', *Art International,* October/ November, vol.21, no.5, pp.42-46

1978:
Daval, Jean-Luc: 'Subject of Contemporary Art: the Image of Nature', *Art Actuel, Skira Annuel,* no.4, pp.93-95, 101
Kultermann, Udo: 'Vermeer and Contemporary American Painting', *American Art Review,* November, vol.4, no.6, pp.114-119, 139-140
Kultermann, Udo: 'Van Gogh in Contemporary Art', *Art Voices South,* November/December, vol.1, part 6, pp.51-55

1979:
Battcock, Gregory: 'Hypocritical Illusions: 3 Artists in New York', *Domus,* January, no.566, pp.53-54
Tatransky, Valentin: 'Malcolm Morley at Nancy Hoffman', *Flash Art,* March/April, no.88/89, p.25
Tatransky, Valentin: 'Malcolm Morley: Towards Erotic Painting', *Arts Magazine,* April, vol.53, no.8, pp.166-168
Whelan, Richard: 'Malcolm Morley', *Art News,* September, vol.78, no.7, p.180 (review of Nancy Hoffman exhibition)
Lawson, Thomas: 'Painting in New York: An Illustrated Guide', *Flash Art,* October/November, no.92/93, pp.4-11
Tatransky, Valentin: 'Malcolm Morley: New Paintings', *Art International,* October, vol.23, no.7, pp.55-59
Lawson, Thomas: 'Malcolm Morley at Nancy Hoffman', *Art in America,* November, vol.67, no.7, p.129

1980:
Hirsh, Linda Baker: 'A Matrix on Innovation'*, *Hartford Advocate,* 16 January, pp.19-20 (review of Wadsworth exhibition)

Kertess, Klaus: 'Figuring it Out', *Artforum,* November, vol.19, no.3, pp.30-35

1980/81:
Tatransky, Valentin: 'Men and their Bodies', *Cover,* Winter, vol.1, no.4, pp.40-45

1981:
Ohff, Heinz: 'Neuer Geist als Explosivestoff', *Tagesspiegel/ Feuilleton,* 18 January, p.4
Levin, Kim: 'Art: Malcolm Morley', *The Village Voice,* 15-21 April, p.64 (review of Xavier Fourcade exhibition)
Mazorarti, Gerald 'Art Picks: Malcolm Morley'*, *The Soho News,* 15-21 April, pp.52-53
Kramer, Hilton: 'A New Wave in Painting: Two Painters Explore New Waves', *New York Times,* Weekend Section, 17 April
Levin, Kim: 'Get the Big Picture'*, *The Village Voice,* 22-28 April (review of Xavier Fourcade exhibition)
Newman, David: 'Malcolm Morley', *Arts Magazine,* June, vol.55, no.10, p.24 (review of Xavier Fourcade exhibition)
Tatransky, Valentin: 'Malcolm Morley', *Arts Magazine,* June, vol.55, no.10, p.2
Kramer, Hilton: 'Expressionism Returns to Painting', *The New York Times,* Arts and Leisure Section, 12 July, pp.1, 23 (review of Xavier Fourcade exhibition)
Russell, John: 'How English Artists Have Come to View New York', *The New York Times,* Arts and Leisure Section, 19 July, pp.1, 25
Castle, Ted: 'The Paint Drain', *Art Monthly,* July/August, no.48, pp.11-13 and cover
Bass, Ruth: 'Malcolm Morley', *Art News,* October, vol.80, no.10, pp.220-222 (review of Xavier Fourcade exhibition)
Levin, Kim: 'Malcolm Morley: Xavier Fourcade', *Flash Art,* October-November, no.104, p.54
Carr, Carolyn Kinder: 'Malcolm Morley: Paintings', *Dialogue, Ohio Arts Journal,* November/December, vol.4, no.1, pp.44-45 (review of Akron exhibition)

1982:
Rose, Barbara: 'Ugly: The Good, the Bad and the Ugly', *Vogue* (U.S.), March, pp.370-375, 425
Nadelman, Cynthia: 'New Editions: Malcolm Morley', *Art News,* April, vol.81, no.4, p.106
Allara, Pamela: 'Issues: New Allogory 1', *Art News,* May, vol.81, no.5, pp.146-149 (review of Boston exhibition)
Renard, Delphine: 'Malcolm Morley: d'un Protoréalisme à Néo-Expressionisme'*, *Artistes,* June/July, no.11, pp.30-34
Saatchi, Doris: 'Artists and Heroes' *Artscribe,* no.37, October, pp.16-19

Chronology

The larger photographs, taken by Steve Moore, show Malcolm Morley at work in his studio, November 1982

1931:
Born in Highgate, London.

Morley never knew his father and in his early childhood he had no settled home. When he was six his mother remarried and Morley adopted his stepfather's name, Evans, which he continued to use until his move to America in 1958. Morley spent much of the war in London, but when the house in which he was living was destroyed by a flying bomb he miraculously escaped injury and was evacuated.

As a child Morley was fascinated by the sea. He made painted balsa wood models of famous ships and on several occasions ran away from home with the aim of going to sea. He eventually served as a galley boy on a tug towing a bucket dredger on a tempestuous voyage to Newfoundland, and worked on North Sea barges.

He spent a year in borstal and subsequently three years in prison and it was there that he developed an interest in painting, beginning a correspondence course in art. On release from prison he took a series of jobs, mainly in the hotel and catering trades and made a visit to Cornwall where he completed a series of topographical watercolours, before being encouraged to pursue a full time course at art college.

1952-53:
Studied in London at Camberwell School of Arts and Crafts, where he continued to paint landscape subjects in the tradition of tonal painting practised by early twentieth-century English painters such as Sickert.

1954-57:
Morley studied at the Royal College of Art, London. He remained a painter of cityscape and landscape and, under the influence of Rouault, of occasional figure subjects. He regarded himself as being rather apart from those contemporaries who were shortly to become associated with pop art, such as Richard Smith and Joe Tilson. In 1956 he saw the exhibition *Modern Art in the United States* at the Tate Gallery. His experience of work by the Abstract Expressionists made him determined to travel to New York. He visited the city in 1957 before returning to London to complete his diploma.

1958:

Morley moved to New York, where he has continued to live with the exception of short periods in Toronto in the late 'fifties, Berlin in 1977, and an eighteen-month residence in Florida in the late 'seventies.

He began to establish himself as an artist in New York, painting during the day or night whilst supporting himself through weekend and evening employment as a waiter on Long Island or in the city. He lived in Brooklyn and in south Manhattan and painted views of Brooklyn, the waterfront and interiors before moving through a phase of painting influenced by Giacometti.

In the early 'sixties these interests in mark and delineation came together with his regard for the work of Barnett Newman and he evolved a form of abstract painting based on the graphic stroke. Working mainly in black and white Morley used a variety of implements, including a pastry gun, to apply the paint, often in flat horizontal bands broken by linear incident in impasto. Later these evolved into stylized land and seascapes. Such paintings were shown at his first one-man exhibition at the Kornblee Gallery in 1964.

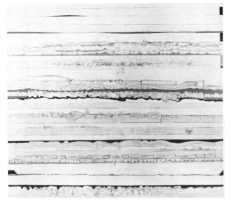

Battle of Hastings 1964

1964-65:

Following the Kornblee show Morley worked on a new series of monochrome paintings, images of battleships and sailors blown up or traced from photographs. An ink wash was flooded over an outline to produce a hazy, looming image with the quality of poor newspaper reproduction. After an attempt to paint a ship from life Morley turned to another printed source – colour postcards and travel agency literature – and adopted the grid technique which has since formed the scaffold for most of his paintings. For Morley at that time the grid had authority through its use by others, such as Richard Artschwager, and it was reminiscent of the traditional practice learned at Camberwell and the Royal College, of squaring up drawings for transfer to canvas.

The grid did indeed assist transfer from the model to the painting, but for Morley its main function was to isolate an area on the model which could then be reconstructed on a larger

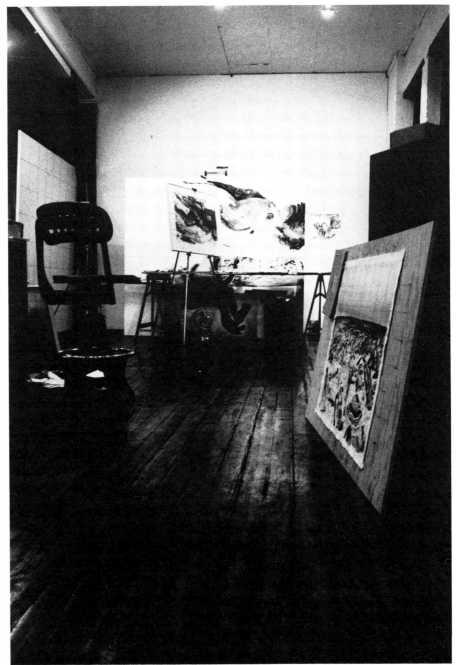

scale on the canvas, without constant reference to its original value within the whole composition. The painter was obliged to invent an alphabet of marks and strokes and to cover the surface evenly, ignoring the traditional hierarchy of figure and ground. Frequently both the model and the canvas were inverted in order to prevent conventional reading and therefore conventional rendering. Most of the paintings for this period have a white border (often cropped in reproduction) which Morley employed so as to reinforce their two-dimensionality and to disclose their source in printed material.

1965:

In 1965-66 he was invited to teach at the State University of Ohio, Columbus, at the suggestion of Roy Lichtenstein, and he has subsequently taught for extended periods at the School of Visual Arts in New York (1967-69) and the State University of New York, Stonybrook (1972-74), as well as giving single lectures and seminars elsewhere.

Throughout the late 'sixties Morley's work was associated and shown with that of the Superrealists (a term invented by Morley) though his practise was quite distinct from theirs, never relying on the projector for enlargement and, through the use of a white border, rendering the conceit of the reproduction evident and ironic.

1971:

In the early 'seventies Morley began to disrupt the 'perfect' surface of his paintings. He achieved this through the use of oils and by the adoption of models which were themselves textured or given an uneven surface through tearing, scraping or crumpling. At the same time the subject matter derived from travel agency literature was gradually abandoned and replaced by invention and more loaded imagery.

During this period Morley began to work, or consider working, in other media and on projects which involved the collaboration of assist-

ants. Several of these works include explicit reference to the work and life of van Gogh. In the early seventies he shot more than eleven hours of film for a project to be called **The Discipline of Vincent, the Ballroom Dancer** and in 1972 he completed a work, **The Last Painting of Vincent van Gogh** in which he simulated van Gogh's *Cornfield with Crows* 1890 and placed it on an easel with a replica gun amongst the paints and brushes in the paint box on the floor.

Detail, taken during the execution of
Los Angeles Yellow Pages 1971

Detail, taken during the execution of **Vermeer, Portrait of the Artist in his Studio,** 1968

76

1972:

Morley was now prepared to consider a more public practice, working outside the studio. In 1972, invited to give a lecture, he dressed himself as Pythagoras and painted one row of the gridded canvas that was to become **School of Athens**.

1973-74

He made several three dimensional paintings including **New York City Postcard Fold-Out,** and a painting, since destroyed, on crumpled sheets of metal, **Hollywood Film Stars and Homes Postcard Fold-Out.** These investigations of the relationship between the third dimension and the flat painted surface led him to incorporate real objects within the paintings, as in **The General** and **SS France** and eventually to the occasional use of three dimensional models and even tableaux observed through a grid stretched in threads across a frame: **Train Wreck** and parts of **The Day of the Locust.**

Hollywood Film Stars and Homes Postcard Fold-Out
1974

1974:

In 1974 he undertook the first of a series of actions which he terms 'social sculpture' and which are designed to test the boundaries of those conventions which define the position and role of the artist within the art world. Invited to take part in an exhibition at the New York Cultural Center Morley submitted a proposal for a painting which by implication would be completed by the artist, with assistance from others, during the course of the exhibition. The work was accepted, but when Morley tried to complete the painting he was ejected and subsequently worked on the painting in a rented truck parked for several weeks outside the Cultural Centre. The painting, was titled **A Painting with Separate Parts which are Self Generating** and incorporates the uncut footage of **The Discipline of Vincent, the Ballroom Dancer.**

Malcolm Morley signing catalogues following his action in Paris, 1974

On hearing that one of his paintings **Buckingham Palace with First Prize** (1970) was to be auctioned in Paris Morley decided that he would 'complete' the painting during the auction. His intention became known to the auction house and when he stepped forward to fire a water pistol paint at the canvas he discovered that it had been wrapped in a protective plastic sheet. Morley, improvising, nailed the gun to the stretcher and the paint escaped, staining the canvas.

1976:

Morley received a commission to paint a work for a chapel in New York City. He arranged for a cross to be fashioned from a large piece of walnut acquired in Texas. This was placed on the back of an assistant and on Good Friday Morley and assistant dressed in tuxedos walked from his studio to the church, stopping at intervals ('stations') to paint the cross.

Paint, Walk, Cross 1976

The paintings shown at the Clocktower, New York, included several showing scenes of disaster or catastophe, incorporating images derived from his earlier paintings juxtaposed with images taken from toy trains and planes.

1977:

Morley spent seven months in Berlin through the German Academic Exchange Programme, but became ill and returned to New York following a period in hospital in Switzerland. In the autumn he returned to the United States and moved in December to Tampa, Florida.

1977-79:

Remained in Florida for eighteen months, making watercolours and paintings. Adopted the practice of using his own drawings and watercolours as the model for works in oil. Paintings may now follow a single watercolour or be composed from several brought together as the painting evolves. Even the toy models are now generally introduced by means of an intermediate watercolour or drawing which may lie unused in the studio for several years before its employment in a major painting. The technique gives Morley freedom to use abrupt changes of scale as a means to disrupt traditional and perceived hierarchies.

1979:

Spent two months in the South of France before returning to New York City.

1980:

Travelled extensively during his first visit to England for more than twenty years.

1981:

Visit to Arizona.

1982:

Visit to Greece and Crete.

Front cover:
Cristoforo Colombo
1965
14x20 (35.5x51)

Back cover:
Macaws, Bengals, with Mullet
1982
120x80 (305x203)
Detail size 14x20 (35.5x51)

Frontispiece:
Malcolm Morley
Photograph by Steve Moore

Edited by Nicholas Serota
Designed by Richard Hollis
Printed in Holland by Lecturis bv, Eindhoven
Photographs by
Anne Gold, Aachen;
Susanne Hilberry Gallery, Inc, Birmingham,
Michigan;
Galerie Jöllenbeck, F. Rosentiel, Cologne;
Prudence Cuming Associates, London;
Bevan Davies, Jonathan Dent
Xavier Fourcade Inc, O.K. Harris Gallery,
Nancy Hoffman Gallery, Bruce C. Jones,
Louis Meisel Gallery, Robert Miller Gallery Inc,
Steve Moore, Eric Pollitzer, Stefanotty Gallery,
Zindman/Fremont, New York;
Munson-Williams-Proctor Institute Museum of Art,
Utica, NY;
Ola Marklund, V Frolunda, Sweden

Published by the Trustees of the Whitechapel Art
Gallery
© 1983 The Authors and Trustees of the Whitechapel
Art Gallery

4,000 copies printed January 1983
ISBN 0 85488 058 5